"Don't let the title of this book fool you. Its purpose is a most serious one—the communication of the timeless truths of our Catholic Faith using images that are compelling to the man or woman of today. Such methods have been with us since the very beginning, ever since Truth made flesh picked up the mustard seed and unveiled to his listeners the power of the grain of wheat. It is my hope and my prayer that many souls will come into contact with this greatest of teachers, Jesus Christ, through the use, study and enjoyment of The Catechism of Hockey."

The Most Reverend
JOHN C. NIENSTEDT
Archbishop of Saint Paul and Minneapolis

"The Catechism of Hockey offers an insightful and unique way of helping readers to better understand their faith. As a bishop and a hockey player, I am grateful for this contribution which I pray will be an effective tool in helping people to grow in a deeper appreciation for the Catholic faith by viewing it through the lens of the game of hockey."

The Most Reverend
THOMAS JOHN PAPROCKI
Bishop of Springfield in Illinois

"Life is hockey? Maybe. The path to greatness is the same for both the NHL and your soul and this book will lead you there."

BRIAN BONIN
1996 Hobey Baker Award Winner

"This book is enjoyable and should be an inspiration to those involved in the game of hockey. Herbie would have been humbled by bringing hockey into the realm of spirituality."

PATTI BROOKS, wife of the late Herb Brooks,
Coach of 1980 USA Men's Olympic Hockey Team

THE CATECHISM OF
HOCKEY

Nihil obstat: Rev. George Welzbacher, *Censor librorum,* Archdiocese of Saint Paul and Minneapolis

Imprimatur: Most Rev. John C. Nienstedt, Archbishop of the Archdiocese of Saint Paul and Minneapolis

LCCN: 2011945191
ISBN: 978-0-9744495-0-0

THE CATECHISM OF
HOCKEY

By Alyssa Bormes

J.M.J.

To Jackie!
Praised be Jesus Christ!

ACS BOOKS

To my beloved parents,
the late William A. Bormes and Karol Bormes Parsons,
who gave me a home,
and
to my beloved spiritual father,
His Excellency, the late Bishop Paul Dudley,
who brought me home.

+ CONTENTS

FOREWORD

By Dale Ahlquist

There is nothing that the new generation pursues more eagerly than this sort of sport and games; and there is nothing that is full of more elaborate restrictions and conditions. But when the same youth attacks the larger problems of life, he has to-day a tendency to do it only with the largest and vaguest theories of liberty, or rather of anarchy. In many cases it is hard to say that he has any philosophy except the philosophy of doing as he likes. Yet the very amusements that he likes most might warn him that the test which breaks down even in little things will be yet more brittle in great ones. He will apply his anarchism to love but not to lawn tennis. Lawn tennis is one network of rules as close as the net itself; and far closer than any of those old Christian nets that were cast by the fishers of men. If there are ten commandments of God there are considerably more than ten commandments of golf. —G.K. CHESTERTON*

Columbia, October, 1924

This is a right wing book. Of course, it's also a left wing book. And a center book. And don't forget the two defensemen and the goalie. The whole team is represented in these pages. Even the referee. And the commissioner. You will think about them all in a new way, even while you think about them in the same way.

What you are holding in your hand is an amazing teaching tool, even though it probably will not help you become a better hockey player. (If that is what you thought you were going to get from this book, well, someone just skated around you. But read it anyway. The game is not over.)

When I met Alyssa Bormes for the first time, she immediately started telling me about this great idea she had called "The Catechism of Hockey." What sounded at first like simply an amusing analogy quickly became a jaw-dropping eternal object lesson. And so I sat there listening to her, open-mouthed, because my jaw had dropped.

"You should write a book," I finally said.

"That's exactly what I am going to do," she grinned, one of those grins that hinted that she had already figured out she was going to write a book even before I brilliantly suggested it.

"I can't wait to read it," I added, scoring another original line.

That was about six years ago. So I *did* have to wait. And I had to remind her a few times about her great idea. In the meantime, I had the pleasure of watching her in action as a teacher, a public speaker, a counselor, a youth leader, and even at times a bookseller. But always a storyteller. Which made me remind her again about her great idea and the book she was going to write. Then I gave her an extra incentive. I told her I would publish it.

So she dug in and set to work. When I read the first draft, I was surprised. I already knew it was going to be about more than hockey. It turned out to be about football and basketball, too.

But it is really about the Catholic Church. That was still the biggest surprise, even though I knew it was coming. And that's the part that will continue to surprise you, even when you know it's coming. You will be surprised by new insights and appreciations. You will be surprised at how incredibly well the metaphor keeps working.

Alyssa has taken subjects that everybody talks about all the time and combined them with subjects that nobody ever wants to talk about. The combination works perfectly. In a world where sports are taken more seriously than religion, and religion is treated more frivolously than a game, she has managed to make a connection between the two that is both serious and fun, bringing back the proper perspective toward each without misrepresenting either. She has found a way to explain the most difficult things to understand about the Catholic Church. She has defended some of the most difficult things to defend. And she has done it by writing about hockey.

Lace up your skates.

INTRODUCTION

The other word for January is "cold." It was another January morning. The sun had managed to show its face for the first time in weeks, and while this did not translate into actual heat, it at least issued an invitation to go outside and take a walk. The brightness was indeed beautiful. The snow seemed to be littered with sparkling diamonds, the air so still and silent that each step sounded particularly *crisp*. There were other familiar sounds of winter. The *sh-sh-sh* of frost being scraped off a windshield. And something wonderfully recognizable to anyone who grew up in the upper Midwest: short, quick, choppy, scraping "footsteps." Then the sleek slicing of blades on the ice, followed by the "footsteps" again. Then another sound that wasn't quite right. Wood slapping…something. I walked on, knowing what I would see. Only one skater, I guessed, and when I arrived at the frozen pond, I saw I was right. A young boy with a funny stocking cap, alone on the ice. The slapping sounds made sense now. He wasn't hitting a rubber puck with his stick. It was a crushed soda can. He wound up and shot it into the goal, a space marked off by two twigs sticking out of two clumps of snow. Although the boy appeared to be alone, he was in fact surrounded by several imaginary defenders, and he weaved between them as he took his shots.

I sat down on a nearby bench and watched. Unaware of me as he maneuvered the crushed soda can with his stick, the young skater continually outsmarted and out-skated the opposition. After another six goals, he stopped. Panting, he took off his funny stocking cap and steam rose from his head into the frozen air. I moved to get up; he looked toward me. We exchanged that sort of Midwestern grin and friendly head nod, and I walked away.

Behind me I could hear the boy begin skating again. I wondered what the score was in his head. This was the sort of hockey that I loved: outside, simple, and pure. My mind began to wander. Without all the trappings, how was I certain this was hockey? Without referees, why did the boy continue to play by the rules? What had been so attractive that I had to stop and watch? Here was something more. The frozen pond and the skating boy were far behind me now, but I could still hear him skating. There came a slap shot, and a yell, "He shoots, he scores!" That was it! The last shot, the goal—finally I understood what I had seen. The boy had been catechized in hockey.

What does that mean? How do "catechism" and "hockey" go together? What are these two words doing together in the same sentence? After all, when we think of the catechism, we think of the Catholic Church. Bingo! (No, I don't mean we think of bingo. I mean, Bingo!) That's the revelation I had when I saw the boy playing hockey on the frozen pond. This is a catechism of hockey, and by understanding it, we can better understand the Catechism of the Catholic Church.

Chapter One

SIMPLY, HOCKEY

The boy on the frozen pond with a stick, a puck, and a pair of skates is playing hockey. Even when he has only twigs for a goal and a crushed soda can for a puck, he is still playing hockey. This is hockey in its rawest form. He embodies the very thing that is hockey—all of the history of hockey, all of its rules, its traditions, everything that hockey ever has been, is, and ever will be. In essence, he symbolizes the whole *faith* of hockey. This all-encompassing *hockey-ness* could be called the *deposit of faith* of hockey.

Perhaps the best thing about hockey is that it is fun, and the sight of one skater on the ice is an invitation for another to join. When the second skater joins the first on the ice, however, rules are needed. Give any two children a puck, a ball, or a deck of cards—or a television remote control—and rules are needed. With a ball, children will quickly make rules governing the number of bounces, the time allotted to hold the ball, boundaries, what constitutes the method of scoring, and a host of other rules. It is the same with the deck of cards, the television remote, and with hockey. Between two young skaters the deposit of faith of hockey remains the same: the rules protect the integrity of the game. One may argue that rules are required even for one skater playing the game of hockey. The rules are implicit for hockey to be hockey, and not another sport.

So, what is hockey? First, in every neighborhood around the world children have made a game of some sort of stick hitting some sort of ball. Parents in every neighborhood around the world hope the stick-hitting-the-ball games are played outside. In certain neighborhoods at a certain time of the year, the weather gets very cold. The children still want to hit the ball with the stick, and the parents still want it done outside.

Second, there is a magical thing about being a child: the love of sliding. When a child slides on the wooden floor or the tiled floor or down the steps, an adult voice in the background tells him to go outside to slide where nothing will be broken. Soon grass stains abound. Water running out of a hose onto a sheet of plastic becomes the epicenter of the town. But sliding is perhaps most exquisite on snow and ice, and flying down a snowy hill on a sled is intoxicating. There is some odd danger in the speed, but the promise of fulfillment is strong, and a spill only encourages more sliding.

But the question remains, what is hockey? It's simple, really. Hockey is the marriage of two dreams of children everywhere: using some sort of stick to hit some sort of ball, and sliding. Hockey came to be in the cold neighborhoods of the world, where the blades of a sled were shortened and put on shoes renamed skates. The stick took on a peculiar "L" shape, and the ball was flattened to become a puck. It's magnificent!

✝

But hockey has become bigger than two children on a frozen pond. For hockey to remain hockey, someone must guard the deposit of faith and articulate the rules. Enter the commissioner and the governing body. They regulate the play of hockey: the make-up of the ice, the lines drawn into it, the boundaries of the rink, the size of the goals, the number of skaters on a team, the equipment worn, and the time allotted—all these are determined by the commissioner and the governing body.

How does this articulation in hockey take place? Consider the helmet. When hockey began, helmets were not a priority. Many of us may still recall professionals who played without helmets. But as our knowledge about injuries to the brain increased, helmets were eventually required for hockey players at every level. This change in equipment did not alter the original deposit of faith; hockey is still hockey. Rather, the commissioner and governing body rightly chose to articulate the rules in a manner that included specific protection for skaters. They added nothing to and took nothing from the deposit of faith. Implicit in the sport of hockey is concern for the safety of the players. Had the authorities not made a rule about the necessity of helmets, they would have been neglectful in their duties. Hockey is meant to be played for more than one day—hockey is for life! It is the job of the commissioner and the governing body to protect skaters so they are free to skate another day.

In the Church there is also a Deposit of Faith, sometimes called the Sacred Deposit. It consists of the entire faith contained in the Sacred Scripture and Tradition. It was entrusted to the whole Church by Jesus Christ and His Apostles.[1] Everything needed for Salvation has already been given to the Church in the Sacred Deposit. This is the Faith of the Church.

Just as hockey has a commissioner and a governing body, so too does the Catholic Church. This authority is known as the *Magisterium* and consists of the bishops in communion with the successor of Peter, the Bishop of Rome, the pope. The task of interpretation has been entrusted to them.[2] It protects the integrity of the Deposit of Faith and articulates the teachings of faith and morals over time.

The Magisterium takes into account developments in the world (including scientific developments), looking at them all through the lens of the Deposit of Faith. It articulates the manner in which one ought to live in current times; if it did not do so, it would be neglectful in its duties.

---

[1] Catholic Church, *Catechism of the Catholic Church.* 2nd ed. (Vatican: Libreria Editrice Vaticana, 2000) 84.

[2] Ibid, 85.

Just as it is logical to have the commissioner and governing body in hockey, and logical that they would protect and interpret the deposit of faith in hockey, so it is logical that the Magisterium of the Church would protect and interpret the Catholic Faith. But the Church is not usually thought of in this way. But what could be more important than protecting the Sacred Deposit? Not only has this Sacred Deposit been protected, but also it is there waiting to be taught, learned, studied, and practiced. By protecting the Deposit, the Church rightly looks after the needs of Her members, providing for them not just in this life, but preparing them for eternal life as well.

Chapter Two

FIRST COACHES

I was just four or five, but I can still remember my father taking me to the rink down the street, a flooded and frozen field with snow at its edges. The day was sunny, and it seemed magical to have strange new boots on my feet. Already wearing his giant brown hockey skates, he finished tying my small white skates. Then he led me to the ice. It seemed easy at first as I stepped from the makeshift bench to the rink. My skates sank into the snow a bit and my feet felt stable; perhaps this skating would be a breeze.

Once on the ice, everything changed. My father held me in front of him with his strong arms, his feet skating to the side of my own. My brothers were near, all of them skating effortlessly. It is still easy to picture their long stocking caps trailing behind them as they raced, glided, and turned, and then stopped quickly.

But my concentration had to remain on standing, and skating. Even with the strength of my father's arms, it wasn't long before I got my first introduction to the cold hard ice. How to keep my feet stable beneath me seemed an utter mystery. Not only did my ankles wobble, but also from time to time I would run into my own feet. Over time, I began to glide on my own. When my father was unable to join us on the ice, my brothers would help me. There was never a time when I felt like an expert; most of my stopping had to do with running into the snow. Never do I remember skating backward, and wide turns involved an inordinate amount of arm-flapping. But I could skate and it was a joy! And forever I will remember my father's giant brown hockey skates to either side of my own small white skates as I looked down at the ice.

✝

Although my father was a hockey player, only one of his eight children pursued the sport. It didn't take long before my parents sent my brother Jerry to one of the disciples of hockey, his first hockey coach.

Every skater is, in a way, a student of hockey. It is to the coaches that we look for a deeper teaching. They were once students; now they are teachers. They are the true disciples of hockey; they are the catechists. They recognize that often the parents are the first teachers of hockey, and the disciples support the good work that is being done at home. They add layers of meaning to the foundation taught at home. The disciple's voice lands clearly on the ear of the skater, and the catechism of hockey continues with a renewed vigor.

There is a certain awe that young skaters feel for the catechist, the coach. Something extraordinary is about to be imparted. The young skaters come prepared to be molded by the disciples, having been instructed by their parents as to the manner in which they are to behave in the presence of the coaches. Especially at the beginning levels, coaches are most often donating their time for the love of hockey and for the love of the children. Compensated or not, coaches are due a particular respect just for being coaches; parents know this. The young skaters are sent to their hockey catechists ready to learn. They arrive early and are prepared to skate at ice time. Once on the ice, they understand they are to listen to the coach and do as the coach instructs. There is to be no idle chatter or disruption; there is no wasting time—ice time or the coach's time.

Imagine the horror of the coach and the other skaters if a young skater were to bring a cell phone onto the ice and begin texting. It goes without saying that there are no cell phones and no texting on the ice. What would the punishment be for that skater? How many laps around the rink? How many push-ups on the ice while wearing 30-40 pounds of equipment? How many *Herbies*? Ah yes, perhaps the most effective yet despised drill named after the beloved Herb Brooks and his coaching technique. Start at the goal line, skate to the blue line, back to the goal line, skate to the red line, back to the goal line, skate to the far blue line, back to the goal line, skate to the far goal line, and back to the original goal line. Then do it again and again, faster and faster, beyond exhaustion. Yes, how many Herbies for texting on the ice?

Would any parent fault the coach for confiscating the phone and handing out Herbies? Would any parent be surprised if all the skaters were doing Herbies when only one skater was texting? This is merely the correction a skater would receive on the ice—imagine the fraternal correction from fellow skaters. Even if another parent drove that skater home, it would be easy to imagine correction taking place during the ride. And then imagine the horror of the parents of the skater. Their very own child acted in a disrespectful manner toward the disciple, the coach. The skater disrespected the team, and disrespected hockey. Imagine the skater's own trepidation while awaiting punishment for the offense. Surely, the cell phone will be lost. Surely, there is a social event that will be canceled, and surely the elderly neighbor has windows that will be washed. Texting on the ice cannot be taken lightly.

The disciples of hockey have earned a certain measure of respect by the very nature of what they do. This respect is not dependent on the level of talent or knowledge of the coach. Instead, coaches are due respect by being coaches. Everyone understands that all skaters must be sent to the disciples, the catechists, ready to skate, ready to listen, ready to believe, ready to act.

There are many disciples, catechists, in the Church. The Pope is a catechist and teaches a catechism lesson each Wednesday at his audience. The priests and religious are catechists; the lay men and women who volunteer at the local parish to teach religious education have become catechists. Respect is due to them for the position they occupy.

Our children must be sent to their catechists on time, ready to listen, ready to believe, ready to act; they must also be sent ready to respect the position of the catechists, the office they hold. Unfortunately, this isn't always the case. Few parents, it seems, are horrified upon being told a child was texting in class or at Mass. Perhaps the parent has even done the same. Often, there is little or no punishment for the offending child. All too often the parent is unconcerned, fraternal correction nonexistent, and the catechist unsupported.

But what if this were hockey? Perhaps it is time to pass out some *spiritual Herbies* to students unprepared to respect the disciples.

Chapter Three

THE TEAM

It was April 5, 2005. We awoke at two in the morning and stopped by the 24-hour bakery on the way to the Vatican. By three, the seven of us were standing on Conciliazione, the street that leads to St. Peter's Square, in line with four million people to view the body of Pope John Paul II.

The line was fifteen to twenty feet wide, marked off by barriers on either side, and so crushing that any movement affected the whole. This may seem like an overstatement, but a friend's story seems to illustrate that closeness well. She was standing further back in the line, and each time she moved her head, she hit the man behind her with the alligator-clip that was in her hair.

Because it was the middle of the night, blankets were passed to whoever needed them by the multitude of volunteers outside the barriers who cared for the pilgrims, those of us standing in line. When a blanket was passed overhead, there was a collective effort to get the blanket to the proper person; there was a sort of mutual understanding to allow it passage. It was much the same during the day as bottled water made the rounds among us.

Although the line was crushing, it was peaceful. The line itself was a prayer. The rosary was prayed in a multitude of languages. There were songs from around the world, and although the verse may have been unrecognizable, it was always a joy when the refrain was a repeated "Alleluia," so we could all join.

The line flowed as one, and we were never certain as to when we would move or stop. Our feet moved collectively with those in front and behind us, and stopped when they stopped. Each time we wanted to move, everyone else had to move. Subsequently, each time someone else wanted to move, we had to move, too. There was even a time when a man probably ten feet behind us began to push his way through to the front. As he approached our left flank, we could hear and feel the collective groaning and movement of the crowd. By the time he reached us, it was incredible how much we had to move in order to let him pass. Yet he was nowhere near us, really.

His pushing was the thing. How grateful I am for his pushing; how sorry I am that he felt he had to push. In him, in the pushing man, I understood the Mystical Body for the first time, and what John Paul II meant when he spoke of there being no private sin. Every movement made in the line affected the rest. If the movements were "good," as in the passing of the blankets, the entire line moved. If the movements were "bad," or "evil," as in those of the man who pushed to get to the front, the entire line moved.

There were others who, since they had "connections," were able to avoid the line; oddly, I felt sorry for them. They had missed the physical and spiritual pilgrimage. Our wait was only a bit more than three hours. Some friends had waited from ten to twenty-four hours. Afterward everyone had the most beautiful stories to tell of waiting in line; the line to see the body of the Holy Father had been a catechism lesson in itself.

Even though we were individuals in that line, we had become, in a sense, one body moving together. In the Church, we are not just physical beings but also spiritual beings, moving together. The unity of spiritual beings is the Mystical Body. In the line, every physical act of "good" or "evil" affected the entire line. In the Church, every spiritual good or evil affects the rest of the Mystical Body. Nothing can be done "privately." Any good act is good for the whole; every evil act, or sin, is bad for the whole. We are all as spiritually close in life as I and four million pilgrims were physically close in the line to view the body of John Paul II.

✝

In hockey, just as in life, there is an analogous body; what is good is good for the body, and what is evil is bad for the body. What is this body in hockey? The team.

If a skater individually performs good acts, then that goodness is good also for the team. This can be true on and off the ice, but is easiest to recognize when the skater is on the ice. For example, if the skater successfully passes the puck, blocks a shot, or scores against the opponent, this is good for the team. Off the ice, if a skater chooses to practice hockey drills at home, or go to a hockey camp, or to eat healthy food, this is also good for the team.

Because the team is the body, however, the skater's "evil" actions affect them negatively. A skater who neglects drills, incurs penalties, or who skates apathetically will negatively affect the team. One might even argue that an apathetic or lukewarm skater is the one of the worst things for the other skaters.

It isn't much harder to see that this is true even when the skater is off the ice. Isn't time spent off the ice solely at the discretion of the skater? When a skater chooses to go to bed at four in the morning before an 8 a.m. game, that decision will affect the team. One individual's poor decision to go to bed at 4 a.m. is no longer private when the rest of the skaters have to compensate for one pair of tired legs.

When a skater chooses to eat a massive meal just before ice time, the team is affected. The "private sin" of that meal will result in a bellyache that could bench the player. The rest of the skaters must work harder in order to overcome the actions of the offending skater.

No matter the examples, they all lead to one truth: there is no private sin in hockey. A skater's individual good action is collectively good for the body, the team. A skater's individual evil action is collectively evil for the body, the team.

Because one skater is part of a whole, there is a certain respect due one's teammates. Any particular good or evil act in hockey certainly does affect that skater, but each action is, in a sense, amplified as it affects the team. In hockey, on and off the ice, a skater is to do good and avoid evil, not only for the sake of the self but for the team as well.

There is no private sin in hockey and there is no private sin in life. The Mystical Body is bound spiritually. It is more tightly bound than a hockey team and more tightly bound than the line to view the body of the Holy Father. Individual good is good for the Church; as is evil, evil for the Church. Every action affects the Church. The members of the Church are to do good and avoid evil, not just for their own sakes, but also for that of the entire Mystical Body.

Chapter Four

THE RULES

If there is to be hockey, there must be rules. Remember the boy on the ice, with skates, a stick, a crushed can, and a few twigs marking off the goal? He was following the rules. Compare him to a child on a field, with cleats, a pointed ball, and a few twigs marking off the goal; this child is also following rules. The child in the first case is following the rules of hockey; the child in the second case the rules of football.

Well, in hockey, there are lots and lots of rules. This thought usually conjures ideas of rules on the ice, however, there are many rules off the ice as well. Oddly these are rarely thought of as rules, but with a quick run through them it can hardly be missed that they are, in fact, rules.

When a family registers a child for hockey, the family receives a schedule of the season with its practices and games. Everything on the schedule is…mandatory. Rarely is there resistance, because the very act of registering for hockey is to make a full commitment to the sport.

There is something about hockey that is a bit different from other sports. It's a little thing referred to as "ice time". Ice rinks, while popular where they exist, are still limited in number. Given the popularity of hockey, the number of teams at every age level, and the limited number of sheets of ice available on which to practice, ice time is at an absolute premium. The family receives a schedule that includes only practices and games arranged…so far. It is understood that the coaches will work to find additional time at the rink. Once this new ice time is procured, it is also mandatory—even if there is only an afternoon's notice.

In addition to the regular schedule and the extra practices, there may also be extra games. Tournaments are added. A winning team qualifies for the winners' bracket. Like everything else, these new games are all mandatory.

In many youth hockey leagues, if a skater misses a mandatory practice the skater is benched for one period of the next game. If a game is missed, the skater is benched for the entirety of the following game. That skater must still be at the game, but is not able to skate. There are consequences for missing mandatory practices and games.

Time at the rink is at a premium, which is why the regular schedule, the additional practices, games, and tournaments all come with an envelope. All ice time costs money, and extra ice time costs extra money, thus, the envelope. At the beginning of the season the family pays for the regular season as scheduled. As new ice time is added families pay, or put another check in another envelope, for their share of that time. As additional games are added, additional money is required.

So in hockey there is a regular schedule that is mandatory. There is extra ice time and games that can pop up at any time and are mandatory. There are consequences for absences, and everything comes with an envelope. What goes in the envelope? A check. Huh—this reminds me of something: the regular schedule, Sundays; extra ice time and games, Holy Days; and it all comes with an offering envelope. Sundays are mandatory. Holy Days are mandatory. They all come with an envelope and there are consequences for absences. Hockey is so Catholic!

Of course we can go to Mass without paying, and some of us squirm when Father even mentions money. But we tithe to hockey. Some of us hemorrhage to hockey. We sacrificially give to hockey, giving until it hurts.

In many youth hockey leagues there is also adult volunteering, and it too is mandatory. At the beginning of the season, in addition to the check given for the regular schedule, a second check is given. Hockey parents often are expected to give forty hours of volunteering to the team per season per child. If they have children in different age groups, the commitment is per child; two kids, eighty hours. A check is given by the parents at the beginning of the season for what the forty hours would be worth. If the parents complete their volunteering commitment, the check is returned un-cashed. If the parents complete part of their commitment, a pro-rated check is returned. If parents do not volunteer their time, the team cashes the check.

These volunteer hours are not a means for parents to decrease the original cost of the season, or a way to supplement the extra ice time or games. The volunteer check is in addition to all the other fees. How does that team keep track of volunteer hours? There is a parent volunteer who monitors these hours.

Imagine how transformative this sort of family volunteer commitment would be for local churches—forty hours per family per year could change the face of the parish. Families working together would come to know each other in a deeper way. Catholics across the generations would meet each other. No longer would parishioners come and go from Mass seeking only to fulfill an obligation. This level of active participation by volunteers would revitalize the parish. The priest would never have to mention it in the announcements again.

But there are lots and lots of rules in hockey, so let's take a look at another. At both games and practice, skaters must arrive early, not just on time for practice, but early. For a practice, it may only be thirty minutes early, with the understanding that skaters are in uniform fifteen minutes before ice time. For games, the norm is forty-five minutes early, with the understanding that skaters will have uniforms on thirty minutes before ice time so they are ready for a pep talk from the coach, followed by a warm-up.

What are skaters doing by arriving early? Preparing themselves physically and mentally for what is about to take place on the ice. The skater takes care in dressing; the pads, breezers, jerseys—sweaters if you are a purist—skates, and helmets are all carefully donned. After the pep talk, the skaters pick up their sticks and proceed to the ice.

If a game is to take place at seven in the evening, the skater counts backward to estimate what time the car must leave the house. A 7 p.m. game necessitates a 6:15 p.m. arrival. The skater likes to meet the rest of the team for some fellowship fifteen minutes before that, making arrival time no later than 6 p.m. If the rink is twenty minutes from the house, 5:40 p.m. The traffic is a bit heavy, so an extra ten minutes is warranted, 5:30 p.m. It is 5:20 p.m. and it is the *skater's* voice that can be heard telling the *parents* to hurry; it is the skater begging to get in the car now. The skater is invested in playing hockey and is the one pushing the family to fulfill the commitment made.

Perhaps there are those parents who think that this sort of earliness is a bit excessive. Why is it necessary? Can't we just skip the fellowship? No, this is of the utmost importance to the skater. The team spends time together in a calm moment before the game; they have time to socialize, to close out the worries of the world and begin the process of preparing for the game. This fellowship time is also a benefit for parents. They have been, in a sense, forced into fellowship by the obligation to get the skater to the rink early. All the parents are early, and enjoy their own time of fellowship.

As the skaters prepare to take the ice, the ritual of donning the uniform gets the blood flowing; each piece of equipment is another reminder of what is to come, the battle for which the skater is preparing. The pep talk from the coach is a call to the spirit and heart of each skater to be present and prepared for the battle, and the sacrifice, in front of them. A good coach calls to his soldiers, his skaters; a great coach not only motivates the team but awakens their youthful energy, in a certain sense, harnessing the team for the task at hand.

With mind ready, the body is next. The skaters take the ice in the warm-up, preparing their muscles for what is to come. Soon they will ask their bodies to fight through exhaustion, to push to a new level, to be one in mind and body, and to face whatever may come in the battle.

In high school, college, and professional games there is even an opening hymn before the sacrifice of the game. It's called the Star Spangled Banner. In hockey, no one who is to take part in the game comes late for the National Anthem. No skater slips onto the ice during or after the opening hymn and expects to play. At that moment, everyone is fully prepared—body and soul—for what is about to take place. When the last notes of the opening hymn have died away, the puck drops and the game begins, and everyone is ready for the glory that is to follow—hockey.

What if we did this before the Mass? What if we encouraged our children to take care to dress for Mass? What if we brought our children early to enjoy fellowship? What if we then spoke to them about what was to take place in the Mass, and what if there were a time of warming up in prayer so they were spiritually ready? What if at the opening hymn our children were ready in body and soul for what was to happen? What if they were *present* for the glory of the Mass?

Yes, the off-ice rules in hockey are far-reaching. There are others having to do with curfews, nutrition, and more. In hockey there never seem to be complaints about the invasiveness of off-ice rules. These rules affect the whole family. Before the season even begins, the parents will have most likely addressed with the child the toll that hockey will exact. Then during the season the true understanding of that commitment is felt. Of course, the parent pushes the child to keep the commitment, but the child is pushing the parent to keep the commitment, too.

Off-ice rules in hockey are not meaningless. They assist skaters in preparing their minds and bodies to be ready for the sacrifice of the game. The Church has rules that reach far beyond the Sacrifice of the Mass, and these rules are not meaningless. Not only do these rules, or commandments, assist the Mystical Body in becoming fully present, body and soul, at the Mass, but also in living life.

Chapter Five

THE BOX

Think again of the boy on that sheet of ice with skates, a stick, a crushed can, and a few twigs marking off the goal; to know that he is playing hockey is to know that there are *on-ice* rules in hockey. Instead of giving a detailed list of the on-ice rules, however, let's turn to what happens when these are broken. When a skater breaks the rules, penalties are assessed. Depending on the severity, *major* or *minor* penalties are imposed. Upon receiving a penalty, the skater goes to *the box*.

Let's say that again: there are *major* and *minor* penalties in hockey and the skater goes to the *box*. *Major* and *minor* and the skater goes to the *box*. I'll pause right here to see if this reminds you of anything. Major, minor, and the box. Mortal, venial, and the *box*. Another name for the box in hockey is the 'sin bin'. Ah! Hockey is so *very* Catholic.

If a skater has to do time in the box, he does his time in the box. In all of hockey history there is no evidence of any skater ever thanking the referee for pointing out the penalty, and then explaining to the ref that he has decided not to do the time now—instead he will save it up and do the penalty time all at once…during Lent. Wow! I wonder how that would go over with the referee? If it were on film it would certainly make every sportscast highlight reel. Then everyone could have a good laugh. "What an idiot! Save it up for Lent—who ever heard of such a thing? Not in hockey."

If a skater has time in the box, that time starts immediately. Any skater refusing to do time is excused from the game. Time is served individually; there may be more than one skater in the box at a time, but skaters are serving their penalties separately. Time in the box is done *individually* and *immediately.*

Perhaps there could be some emergency in hockey that would necessitate the whole team taking time in the box together. But in all of hockey history, there has never been mention of this—all together in the box, for all the penalties received in a game or season—it has never happened. Though everyone has to do his own time in the box, penalties still affect everybody.

In hockey, there are five skaters and one goalie per team that can be on the ice at a time. When a given team has all five skaters and the goalie on the ice at once, they are considered to be playing at *full strength.* Time in the box removes a skater from the ice, and no skater from the bench is sent in to replace the missing skater. This is considered skating *shorthanded.*

Upon receiving a penalty, a skater forces the body, the team, to play shorthanded. Upon completion of the penalty time, however, the skater returns to the ice. If no other skaters are in the box, the team is now skating at full strength. In certain situations, penalty time ends if the opposing team scores against the shorthanded team. This event also returns the shorthanded team to full strength.

At the Minnesota Gopher games, after a penalty is over, the announcer says, "The Gophers are at full strength."

The crowd responds, "They always were!"

I once told this to my friend Fr. Paul Murray. He gasped and whispered, "Yes. Say it again."

"The Gophers are at full strength."

"They always were."

"Yes, that's it, that's confession."

After penitents have done their time in the *box,* they are at full strength. God's forgiveness is *complete.* The offense is gone; in a sense, it is as if it never happened. There may still be *temporal* consequences, however, that need to be remedied. Spiritually, the sin may be gone, but the consequences of the sin may remain.

In hockey, penalty time is considered complete when time runs out on the penalty or, in some cases, when the opposing team has scored. The offense is past, the time in the box is done, and all has been forgiven. But because of the penalty the skater forced the body to play shorthanded. When the skater returns to the ice, these temporal consequences remain and must be remedied. The team is tired from having to play one skater short, thereby increasing their workload against the opposing team. If the penalty ended because the team was scored against, the temporal consequences of this are no small matter. But the penalty has been fully expiated in the box and it is as though the team has always been at full strength.

+

"The Gophers are at full strength."

"They always were."

Imagine if, for even one day, we as the Church played at full strength! If each of Her members were in a state of grace, the world would be transformed.

There is no shame in the box. You are not at your worst when you are in the box. You are at your worst when you are sinning. One might even say that you are at your best when you are in the box. You come humbly before Christ. You tell the Divine *Referee* your transgressions and you are met with Mercy Himself.

If you have time to do in the box, do your time in the box. Don't make the team play shorthanded because you are afraid of the box. The box is just a part of hockey, and it is just a part of the Church. Go do your time in the box.

"The Church is at full strength."

"She always was!"

Chapter Six

IN THE BOX

Hockey is merciful. Yes, hockey is utterly merciful. This is not to say that it is easy, or even to say that it is not physical. Hockey is very difficult and very physical, but it is still merciful. Implicitly and explicitly, the deposit of faith of hockey is full of rules, which have been articulated by the commissioner and the governing body. Each skater is aware of the rules and is to play under the rules. This is merciful. The rules are the rules; they govern the game. They don't change on the whim of the referee, the coach, or even the skater. Skaters know how to behave on the ice, and, in order to ensure this, there are referees who witness each game. Their role is to make certain that the rules are followed. They are the ones who call the penalties; they are the ones who excuse the players to the box.

But if the skater is sent to the *penalty* box, how can hockey be merciful? Even the name of the box points out the failure of the skater, the penalty. Beyond that, the team is made to play shorthanded. Where is the mercy? And where is the mercy in having someone point out your faults all the time? Wouldn't it be more merciful not to call penalties?

Everyone in hockey recognizes the box as a part of hockey. It seems that the only argument with the box comes when the penalty is called. As an indication of how well-connected the body of hockey is, a fan may be just as upset about the penalty as the skater. At other times, skaters and even fans may be resigned to a penalty. "Yep, that penalty was deserved."

If penalties were not called, there would be an uproar. If referees were blind to penalties, the game would become inordinately more dangerous. We expect that referees will call penalties and that offending skaters will be sent to the box. Yet all this identifying and paying for penalties doesn't exactly come across as mercy.

The *penalty* box may more aptly be named the *mercy* box. There is a cleansing and a healing that takes place. How does it happen? As the seconds tick away and the penalty nears its end, the skater prepares to skate again, penalty-free. The team prepares to play at full strength.

At what point in the box is the healing complete? It's not over until it's over, but even taking that into consideration, there is still a shift, a movement toward wholeness. Everyone—the skater, the team, the fans—everyone is waiting for the time to end. Even before the last seconds of the penalty, the excitement increases. A bridge has been crossed, hope abounds.

"The Gophers are at full strength."

"They always were!"

Everyone understands that the penalty is gone; it no longer exists. What happens in the box is transformative. The skater enters the box with a penalty, but leaves without one. At some point in the box, the skater met mercy. How? When? In a certain sense, it's a mystery.

Perhaps one of the most mysterious practices in the Catholic Church is the Sacrament of Confession. Nearly everyone has seen *the box* in movies, but that only seems to further veil the mystery. In the movies, the priest is often just a voice, deep and foreboding, behind a screen. At other times confession is portrayed as a caricature of itself: ridiculous, unnecessary, and often offensive. At these times it seems Catholics in the audience laugh the loudest. Is this because we don't take ourselves too seriously, or do we see confession as ridiculous and unnecessary?

Even the name confessional seems ridiculous. Confess—as in, to say what you did wrong? Great, just what Catholics need, another means by which to feel guilty. Go to the box and admit your faults in order that someone can make you feel terrible about yourself. It's no wonder that there are no lines at the box anymore.

As for meeting mercy in the box, it seems that the only meeting now taking place is the one with guilt. Wouldn't it be more merciful to let people do what they want? Why should we have to dwell on our faults? Not to mention, who has the right to point out my faults? But it comes back to the rules. You can't play the game if you don't follow the rules.

The Deposit of Faith is full of implicit and explicit rules that the bishops in union with the Pope articulate. To be Catholic is to be aware of the rules and to play under the rules. The rules are the rules—they govern life. If the rules are ignored, life becomes inordinately more dangerous. It's not just men in collars who point out broken rules, or sins. Parents point out sins to their children all the time. It's their duty. Those in authority neglect their office by not calling sin by its name. The work of authority is to articulate what sin is; personal maturity is being able to see sin in your own heart without having it pointed out.

What is amazing is that the Church has never *hidden* the box. Everyone knows about the box; it's one of the Big Seven, as in the Sacraments. Every Catholic agrees there are seven Sacraments *corporately*, but the number of Sacraments that pertain to the *individual* seem to be up for discussion. Confession, in particular, is often seen as optional. "Sure, I can see why other people might need a box to air their dirty laundry, but for me, it's unnecessary." Questioning the box is just a way to put off going into the box.

When I am not playing at full strength, the mystical body, the Church, is not playing at full strength. To rectify my weakness, I take a trip to the box. So what happens in the box? All I have are my experiences to share, but perhaps there is something to be learned.

✝

When I was a child my parents took me to the Sacraments. I was seven years old when they took me to confession for the first time. But then they did something radical...*they kept taking me!* They didn't mention it at the time, but it was as if they were saying, "If you ever get lost, this is the road map home."

Think of a child who is making a first trip alone to the neighbor's. The child has been led by the hand a hundred times to and from the neighbor's house and now it is time for the first solo outing. By phone, the neighbor is alerted of the child's coming. The parent watches the child depart as the neighbor awaits the approach. When the child reaches his destination safely, another call goes back to the parent reporting this. The process will be reversed in a few hours. Later, the child goes off to a first sleepover. The parent reminds the child to call at anytime of the night and the parent will come. In either case, the child knows the way home. As the child grows and takes longer and longer journeys, there is always the road map. Should a young child be left to wander alone, the parent would be held responsible.

The spiritual life is the same. The continual trips to the confessional with my parents and at my school were constant reminders of the way home.

"Someday you may be lost, and this is the road map home."

"Someday you may not be able to find us, but this is the road map home."

"Someday you may be so lost that we cannot even find you and you will no longer think that you can reach us, but this is the road map home."

"Find the collar."

"Wherever you are in the world, however lost you are, come home, this is the way, find a priest and go to confession, and you will be home."

For seventeen years I was utterly lost. So lost, I didn't even know I was lost. So lost, I couldn't hear the voices of my parents calling me home. But there was a day when it was so black that I couldn't help but see the map. I had to go home.

And so I called Bishop Paul Dudley, of happy memory. He invited me to his home. "Bless me Father for I have sinned. It has been seventeen years since my last confession." I told him every last thing, every last sin. At the end, in his gentle, beautiful voice he said, "Alyssa, imagine the rejoicing in heaven today for one sinner coming home." In a single breath, he welcomed me *home*. But I would have never gotten home if my parents had not given me the road map.

When I was leaving, Bishop Dudley stopped me in the doorway. This time there was a firmness added to his voice. He emphatically said, "Alyssa, God has forgiven you. Now, go home and do the hard work of forgiving yourself." I had no idea that forgiving myself was required. But his words rang in my head and finally I did it.

You must give your children the road map home—if you do not, you will be held accountable. Will your adult children use the road map home? Maybe, maybe not, but they must at least *have* the map if they are ever to use it.

The box is a place of healing. Get in the box and get yourself some mercy!

Chapter Seven

MINI MITES, MITES, AND SQUIRTS

The phone would ring, a parent would be on the line, and serious conversation would follow. The parent was telling me that his or her second grader was not ready to receive First Reconciliation. The usual reason was that the child was too young to really understand right from wrong.

As the parish Faith Formation Director, my response was gentle and measured each time, "Okay, you are the first teacher of Teresa. No one would understand this more than you. Thank you so much for letting me know this, as we don't want children to receive the Sacraments before they're ready." Following this was a question as to when the child would be ready. The usual response: "In a year or two." My reply was always agreeable: "Great, then that is what we will plan on, please let me know when she is ready and we will prepare her at that time. Then later that following spring, she will receive her First Communion."

Every single time came a breathy "What?" from the parents. They wanted their children to receive communion with the rest of the second graders in the spring.

I would then verify with the parent that there were no mental disabilities, because that could change everything. "No, no disabilities with my Teresa. But why does she have to wait for her First Communion?"

"Barring a problem like a disability, the children are to receive reconciliation before communion. Because you are the first teacher, you know better than anyone if Teresa *understands* right from wrong. We respect that."

Then I would usually say something along the lines of, "Can I ask you something completely off the topic?"

"Yes."

"Did I see that Teresa is on the soccer team?"

"Yes, she is."

"How is she doing?"

"Great, they just won a game last week."

"By now they are playing positions, right?"

"Yes."

"How is she doing at her position?"

"Great, she really seems to like offense and even scored a goal earlier in the season."

"Fantastic, so she really has the rules down—even understands the penalties."

"Yes."

"So she knows right from wrong...in soccer."

By now the parent was beginning to see where the conversation was headed. A resigned "Yes" came through the line.

"So Teresa has the capacity to know right from wrong in soccer because those rules were taught to her, but she is unaware of what is right and wrong in life? Since she has the capacity to know right from wrong, it seems that she just needs to be taught the rules in life."

These conversations rarely continued much further, but every single time parents agreed they would have their children coming to me for reconciliation classes with the other second graders. Not once was a parent upset with me. They came to understand through a simple parable that their children did know right from wrong.

Children know right from wrong very early; watch them with a ball, or on a soccer field, or on a sheet of ice. They know the rules; they know right from wrong. We teach them the rules in sports.

Further, we *expect* them to know the rules of soccer or hockey or football. Perhaps we should teach them and expect them to know the rules, right from wrong, in life.

✝

In hockey, as in most sports, the youngest children are separated by age. In their earliest years, the goal is to teach the children how to skate, and to teach them the rules. The very youngest hockey teams are called Mini Mites, then the following year called Mites. It is not until they reach eight to ten years old, when they are in Squirts, that they are skating competitively. Once they are in Squirts, the box comes into play. Squirts skaters have spent time learning the early hockey catechesis of Mites and Mini Mites. The rules of hockey have been drilled into them. As Squirts they are now responsible for the penalties they commit.

It is the same in the Church. Young children are taught right from wrong over a course of years. Although the age may fluctuate some depending on the child, usually, seven years old is considered the age of reason. It is at this time that they begin to be responsible for their actions, good and bad. It is at this time that they are introduced to the confessional, the *box*. As parents, we understand that bad actions result in penalties on the hockey field, on the soccer field, on the basketball court, and in nearly every other sport. As parents, we should also understand that bad actions are sinful. It is the box in both hockey and the Church where everything is rectified.

✝

As a side note, I have a special request of parents. Think of the first time your child receives Communion. What do you say? "Are you excited?" "It will be the best day of your life!" "Who will you be receiving?" And after they receive their First Communion, we ask,

"How was it?" "How do you feel?" "Wasn't it great?" "I bet you can't wait to receive Communion again!" A few weeks after that, "How many times have you received Communion?" "Do you know you can receive during the week as well?"

But when we speak to the children about Confession, we say things like, "Are you nervous? I'm petrified of Confession." "I wouldn't even know how to go to Confession anymore!" Then after their First Confession, we say things like, "Was it scary?" "Was Father mean?" And if someone offers to take them to confession again, we hear, "Oh, they don't have to go again so soon, do they?"

Both Sacraments, Confession and Communion, are meetings with Christ! Why would we ever want to keep our children from meeting Christ?

I'll never forget the first children I prepared for Reconciliation. I asked them to come to the front of the aisle in the church, but forgot to tell them to stay in two lines while waiting for the next available confessor. What I had was forty second graders elbowing their way to be first, or next, in line for confession. Mentally, I made a note to remember to tell the next forty children, who would be there a short hour later, to stay in two lines.

More than one parent came to see me after the first group of children had made their First Confession. To say the least, I was nervous about their comments, as they had witnessed the fracas.

Then came the unexpected: "I love what you did with the kids!"

My reply was tentative, "What do you mean?"

"The part of having them come to you as a group."

Not understanding, I replied with a questioning, "Oh?"

"It was amazing to see that none of them were nervous to go to confession. They wanted to go. It is just us, as adults, who make them nervous because *we're* so nervous."

From then on, there was always a little elbowing and a little fracas as my students waited impatiently for their confessors. I did my best to keep order, but there was just something a little beautiful about seeing one child's shoulder move in front of another's in hopes of getting to confession first. The children were little evangelists who couldn't wait to meet Christ in the Sacrament.

So my request to parents is, teach your children about meeting Christ in all the Sacraments. Don't ask them if they are nervous or frightened just because you are. Don't keep them from Confession or the Eucharist; let them make the habit when they are eager to do so. Your children have a longing for the Sacraments; they have a longing to meet Christ there. Let their longing soften your hearts.

Chapter Eight

HIGH STICKING AND SLASHING

At a baby's baptism, there is tremendous joy. The parents, godparents, aunts and uncles, and even the community have the highest hopes for the baby's future. May the baby live the *best* life possible! May the baby always be close to Christ and His Church!

Think of how many fathers say, "She won't date until she's thirty." Or a mother who says, "I hope he stays interested in cars and trucks until he is twenty-five." Certainly, these are said with a light-hearted humor. But why this light-heartedness in the first place? The parents see the purity of their child. They see the innocence. They want only the best for the child.

If parents were asked at the baptismal font if they wanted their child to be married in the Church and to approach the Sacrament of Marriage as a virgin, they would say yes. They are holding perfection in their arms; they desire only the best for their beautiful, innocent child.

And so the catechesis begins. The child has a Noah's ark on the wall of the nursery and a crucifix above the crib. The child begins to learn of Jesus, Mary, and Joseph, begins to go to Mass. The parents assist the child in learning prayers and the Sign of the Cross. The child begins to learn right from wrong. The catechesis is fully taught according to the age of the child.

Something begins to happen as the child becomes a teenager, however. There is often a *backing away* from catechesis. At first it is barely noticeable, but the slide down the slippery slope has begun. Suddenly a child begins to skip Mass in high school. The parents say, "Well, I can't really say anything because I used to skip Mass in high school." The teenager begins to binge drink, use drugs, and experiment sexually. And the parent says, "Well, I can't really say anything because I used to (fill-in-the-blank) when I was her age."

After the great hope for the *best* possible life of purity and communion with the Church on the day of baptism, the catechesis has somehow fallen off the cliff. Is it that the Church has unrealistic expectations? No. I argue that there are two things at work: unresolved sin and a conspiracy of silence.

✝

Take for example John, who is now a hockey parent. In high school John had a problem with carrying the stick above the opponent's shoulders, which is called high sticking. It is dangerous and against the rules. John's high sticking normally resulted in minor penalties, but there were a few times when he injured another skater and was assessed a major penalty. John did plenty of time in the box. Eventually, his high sticking ways were harnessed by time in the box, reprimands from the coach, and fraternal correction from the team who had to skate shorthanded often because of him. In addition, John was really affected by the last injury he caused. Finally, he resolved his *sin* of high sticking.

John now has a child, Rachel, who has a similar high sticking problem. What are the chances that John would now say, "Well, I can't really say anything to Rachel about her high sticking because I did it in high school"? Instead, John would be the most emphatic voice in Rachel's life against high sticking. Why? Because John resolved his sin of high sticking, he is now eminently qualified to speak to her about it. John did his time in the box. He knows how high sticking affects the body of hockey, and he has seen the damage and danger of high sticking as it pertains to those whom he hit.

Not only would John be a powerful voice to Rachel against high sticking, but he would also expect the referees, the coaches, and the team to correct her. He wouldn't coddle her when she got caught high sticking and had to do time in the box. Instead he would point out that *sin* has *consequences*. He would not hesitate to catechize her about the ills of high sticking. Had John never resolved his problem, never done the time in the box, never taken correction, it would be no surprise when he didn't correct his own daughter.

Imagine the reaction of other parents if they heard John saying, "I can't say anything to Rachel because I used to do the same thing in high school." They would surely call John on the carpet. "Grow a backbone!" "Put your foot down!" "Say something!" "You cannot let this go on—it's too dangerous!" "Do you care nothing for your own child's safety and the safety of those around her?"

It would be a scandal. John, who never came to grips with his own sin, now has no backbone to help his daughter out of hers. He has quit hockey catechesis as a result of not having resolved his own failing. What a shame. What a shame for John, what a shame for hockey, what a shame for Rachel.

John had such great hopes for his daughter when he taught her to skate while holding her in front of him, with his skates on either side of hers. She was going to live, breathe, sleep, dream, and play hockey. Instead, he has given up on the catechesis of hockey and in turn given up on Rachel.

Unresolved sin leads to a sort of *death*. Hockey is about life, but Rachel has taken a path against life and against hockey; her hockey heart is becoming hardened. Hockey may soon be dead to Rachel. Rachel will do what she wants to do when she wants to do it. Her concern is no longer about hockey; it is about Rachel, about the self.

+

Unresolved sin leads to a death of catechesis; so does the conspiracy of silence, and they both lead to a turning inward on the self. In John's case, he never resolved his sin of high sticking; therefore he never had the wherewithal to catechize his daughter, leaving her in danger. It's not that John disagrees with hockey's teaching on high sticking; rather he does not want to admit his fault, his sin.

In contrast, the conspiracy of silence is often the product of a radical dissent from teaching. The parent involved in a conspiracy of silence may have played hockey as a youth, may not have, or may even have been a convert from a basketball family. The experience of being a skater is not the important thing—the dissent from teaching is. Let's take the case of Olivia. She is a hockey parent, having never played as a youth, but was always a faithful fan of hockey and its teachings, except in one thing—slashing. Slashing is misuse of the hockey stick, swinging it at the opponent, it is against the rules, and can be dangerous.

Olivia is happy that her children are hockey skaters and has hopes for their success. She wants her children to live, breathe, sleep, dream, and play hockey, and does whatever she can to support them, except to warn them about slashing. She knows that slashing is against the rules but has never really understood why. She feels that slashing could have a place in hockey, and doesn't understand why the commissioner and governing body don't get with the times and eliminate the slashing penalty.

Olivia picked a team for her son Jason based largely on the fact that the disciple, the coach, had the same hockey views as she did. Coach Brown doesn't exactly mention his views on slashing and would never teach against the rules of hockey, but his silence on slashing is as good as any endorsement of it. Other parents have sent their children to Coach Brown for similar reasons.

Jason's hockey catechesis has been complete except where it pertains to slashing. He never checks from behind because it is just wrong. He is known as an advocate of good sportsmanship, and he is always very attentive at the opening hymn, the National Anthem.

But Jason stumbles at slashing. Skaters from other teams have mentioned to him that it is against the rules, but he has always felt that these skaters were stifled by their overzealous parents and coaches.

Jason now has a slashing habit, and because no one close to him—parents and coaches and other skaters—seem to care, his habit has been reinforced. He has even overheard his coach and some of the parents complain that the commissioner doesn't have any business interfering in the management of their rink. Jason knows how to *act* as if he doesn't approve of slashing when he is around those who disagree with him, but deep down Jason feels that slashing is just the wave of the future in hockey, and it is just a matter of time before hockey gets the *right* commissioner and the rule changes. So Jason continues with slashing.

Having the *right* commissioner will not matter, because slashing is wrong. Hockey is hockey. The commissioner and governing body are there to protect and articulate the rules, the deposit of faith. They are not concerned whether slashing is trendy; neither do they seek to please rogue skaters or want to give them a false-relief from guilt. They are not willing to sacrifice the safety of the skaters to make a faction happy. Hockey is for *life*. The skaters' safety is of the utmost importance. The rule on slashing won't change.

But Coach Brown and Olivia and other like-minded parents have become their own *commissioner*. And their silence is deafening. Jason will come to accept to slashing. If those around him choose by their silence to endorse slashing, then Jason will slash. Perhaps slashing will become the hockey norm. Everyone is doing it, therefore it must be right. If those around Jason remain silent, he will be catechized by *someone*. The world around him will catechize him instead, and its voice will seem very loud indeed in the silence of the truth. Jason's heart will eventually harden to any mention of slashing as wrong. He won't even pretend that it is wrong anymore when in certain crowds. Slashing is the way it is; get over it!

There will come a day when Jason will get *caught* slashing, however. Not only will he incur penalties, but Jason may also inflict damage that cannot be undone because of slashing. He may wonder why no one ever taught him about its ills. He saw it in the rulebook once, but was told it was an unimportant trifle. Ah—what a shame for Jason, what a shame for Olivia, what a shame for Coach Brown and the other silent voices, and what a shame for hockey.

One day Jason may reflect on his time in hockey, and see the damage slashing has done to him, to his team, and to other skaters. He may come to understand the wisdom of the commissioner and governing body and their articulation of the rules. He may break the conspiracy of silence. He may go on to catechize others on the hazards of slashing, but that would make him a rare exception.

Too often skaters in Jason's position can't even see the connection between slashing and the swath of damage around them. They maintain the conspiracy of silence, and catechize others with it, or offer radical vocal dissent against the commissioner and the governing body while maintaining a "faithful" posture—they are catechizing the way they think it *should* be. Jason is unaware that his radical dissent is no longer about hockey, but is now about the self. Jason's attempt to breathe life into his dissent is spreading death to hockey.

✝

Hockey is *alive*. Unresolved sin and the conspiracy of silence do nothing to promote hockey. Instead, they lead to a *perversion* of hockey, which is not real hockey at all and will eventually lead to the *death* of hockey.

High sticking is high sticking, slashing is slashing, and sin is sin—none of these are ever right. John is not obligated to tell Rachel of his high sticking in high school, but he is obligated to direct her away from it. In the same way, parents are not obligated to tell the sins of their youth to their children, but they are obligated to direct their children away from sin. Olivia and parents like her do nothing to assist Jason when she is silent in the face of sin.

Unresolved sin and the conspiracy of silence do nothing to promote the teachings of the Catholic Church. Well-meaning parents, teachers, and pastors do nothing for youth when they ignore dissent, thereby ignoring the damage that may be inflicted upon youth. Silence on difficult Church teachings is not compassionate parenting, nor is it pastoral. The conspiracy of silence is a shame for the children, a shame for the parents and pastors, and a shame for the Church.

A *perversion* of Catholic teaching is not Catholic teaching. Catholic teaching *reflects a living truth*. Unresolved sin and the conspiracy of silence lead to a loss of innocence. The hopes we held for our children at baptism must not be discarded because of our unresolved sin and our deafening silence. Sin, even if everyone is doing it, is a *death*. It's time to choose *life* for our children!

Chapter Nine

NEVER IN HOCKEY

Coach Anderson is catechizing her skaters and a question arises about off-side. Coach has been skating since she was a child and remembers when she first learned about off-side. She feels almost nostalgic for a moment, and remembers the many disciples that she learned from, all their hard work, and all their good intentions. When she was a child, off-side was perhaps *over* emphasized and it felt a bit stifling. She is grateful that she is now able to catechize in a manner that allows for the skaters' personal freedom.

Coach Anderson closes her eyes for a moment and breathes deeply, aware of what a transformative time we live in. Oh sure, there are still some hold-outs, but luckily most of the disciples think as she does. When she opens her eyes, she looks into the bright eyes of her young skaters and begins to explain, "Although off-side is still on the books, it is an old teaching and we don't really have to follow it anymore. The commissioner and governing body just haven't gotten around to changing it *yet*. Maybe some of you with older parents have been told about off-side; they may even have stressed its importance. With all due respect to your parents, who were your first teachers of hockey, off-side is antiquated and has nearly nothing to do with hockey as we know it today. If some of you skaters would still like to practice off-side, you are more than welcome to; there is room for you in hockey as well. But under my direction, we will not be learning about off-side."

"But Coach, my parents really feel that off-side is still important and they were hoping you could expand the teaching for me."

"I'm not saying this just to you, but to all my skaters here today: If your parents want to teach you about off-side, I will not dissuade them and I will not make you do otherwise. But let's remember that you are now able to make choices and hockey is much different than in your parents' day. I know, I lived through it—and luckily I have overcome it. Let's not worry about off-side. Now, I think you all have had your say, so let's mark this off the list and not revisit it again. Let's get on to what hockey is really about. And besides, we have a big tournament in front of us, let's put all the nonsense aside and get ready!"

✝

Across town, Coach McCarthy has his skaters doing drills. The skaters complete their last three *Herbies*; he blows the whistle, and they meet him at center-ice. He has a policy for the last five minutes of practice: bring your questions. At the beginning of the season, the skaters usually didn't know what to ask, so Coach assigned skaters to come up with questions. As the season progressed, however, the skaters got the hang of it and were no longer self-conscious. The questions came freely, and today was just such a day.

"Coach, my cousin from the Iron Range was telling me about icing. I didn't really get it, but I tried to act like I did. What is it?"

"Icing-*Schmicing!* Don't worry about it, kid, icing is a matter of conscience and you can just do what your conscience dictates." Ah, Coach says bad things so well. He blew his whistle and practice was over. "See you at the tournament." The skaters still don't know what icing is, but at least they know they don't have to worry about it.

✝

After a quick (or not so quick) Zamboni run, the ice is smooth again and Coach Hanson ushers her team onto the ice. This woman plays by the book! She is tough and skaters quickly learn after a few too many wall-sits that she means business.

A mom of one of the skaters is *actually* friends with Coach Hanson. The skaters can't quite believe it, but at least the team has found out her first name…Ruth. More than once, under the breaths of the skaters, as they were lined up around the rink with their backs against the boards and their knees bent like a chair, the whisper could be heard. "Ruthless." It was the only thing that got them through as she yelled, "Lower!"

Yep, Hanson goes by the book; she even brings it with her to practice each day. Today she blew the whistle and then barked, "We're going to learn about the goalie's area, the crease." She went through the entire catechism with each skater. She pointed at diagrams in the book, and had handouts ready with a three-hole punch so they could be put right into each skater's binder. She went over and over the fact that the skaters could not enter the goalie's crease and interfere with play. Then she made a final proclamation, "We always follow the rules—and we don't go into the crease to interfere with the goalie!" (Wink, nod.) "Now get some sleep tonight before the big tournament tomorrow." Coach Hanson left the ice.

A wink and a nod? Did Coach really just teach that whole thing with a wink and a nod? As you can imagine, the skaters were frozen in a stunned silence. What just happened? Finally, a first skater spoke, "So are we supposed to go into the crease and interfere with the goalie or not?" This broke open a discussion. Some skaters didn't see the wink and nod, so they couldn't be sure. Others didn't know what the wink and nod meant. One astute skater spoke about his grandpa who was a jokester and did everything with a wink and a nod. It was that skater who was able to crack the code for the rest and break the good news, "When someone uses a wink and a nod, it undoes everything else they just said! We don't *have* to stay out of the crease! We can get right in there and go after the goalie!" Maybe ole' Ruthless wasn't that bad.

The clock just hit 10 p.m. Coach Phillips was lucky enough to get ice-time on a Friday night before a tournament. While his assistant coach collected checks from the parents for the extra ice-time, Coach Phillips led his skaters in some warm-ups. Coach was *such* a good skater; he had skated all the way through college.

Understandably, the kids were nervous before their first big tournament. A particularly nervous skater would always revert back to some of the old hang-ups. Coach saw it coming and headed it off at the pass: "Don't let your disagreement with the rule against charging keep you from playing hockey!" Disaster averted; practice finished. "Replenish your liquids tonight, lay off the sweets, get some sleep, wake up early for a high-protein breakfast, don't forget some carbs, and I'll see you here at 8 a.m."

Old teaching, not changed *yet*, a matter of conscience, teaching with a wink and a nod, and not worrying about a disagreement with established doctrine—this would *never* happen as skaters are being catechized in hockey. The rules are the rules, and they are taught with an eye to the whole, to hockey itself.

Imagine the outrage of hockey parents whose children have been told that the teaching on off-side hasn't been changed, *yet*. The off-side rule isn't going to change. To say *yet* implies that it *is* going to be changed. The disciple who taught this would soon find herself without anyone to catechize; even tenure wouldn't save her job. No, this would never be done in hockey, but it is nearly expected when our children are being catechized in the Faith. And worse, it is often accepted and even rewarded.

Imagine if Coaches Anderson, Hanson, McCarthy, and Phillips and their teams were to compete against each other at the big tournament. The games would have the appearance of hockey, but in short order fall into chaos. Anderson disagrees with off-side, but she holds fast to the teaching on icing. When her team meets McCarthy's team, in just minutes there would be disagreement over the rules. It would be much the same for Hanson and Phillips. In addition the referees might have their own twisted idea of the rules. Such a tournament may *resemble* hockey, but a *perversion* of hockey is not hockey. Once the rules, *the teachings*, of hockey fall, then hockey falls.

Hockey is beautiful. Skaters from opposing teams come together on the same sheet of ice, with the same rules, and begin the game. Hockey reveals its beauty in sanctioned, uniform play. Chaos may hold our interest for a short time, but it soon becomes tedious; chaos causes uneasiness. It is loud, and to be honest, it's ugly.

In hockey, there must be uniformity in teaching. This is not to say that there cannot be different styles. Even on a single team there are different styles. One skater may have a long, beautiful, fluid stride. Another skater has a short, choppy, utilitarian hustle. The goalie and the defenseman, by necessity, have vastly different styles.

While the coaching staff may change, uniformity must remain constant. A skater moves from one age group to the next, and may encounter many different coaches. There are periodic staff changes at all levels of hockey, including those of the commissioner and governing body, but the message is still the same. Hockey is still hockey. From arena to arena, a goal must remain a goal, and a penalty remain a penalty. The deposit of faith of hockey remains intact through uniformity in teaching and practice; this insistence on order allows hockey to achieve its full beauty.

Beauty depends on order. Freedom, variation, excitement, and surprise all exist within the rules; without the rules, there is only chaos. A particular friend gave very pointed advice about chaos and order. Here is the same advice revamped for the young skater and the young catechumen.

Advice to a young skater: God bless you and persevere in your hockey catechesis, which is forming you by disciplining all your thoughts and actions so that the ultimate presentation of them is in the greatest service to hockey. Remember, it is not hockey if it is chaos. Hockey is a sport of order. All the thrills come when everyone is playing the game at their highest level according to the rules.

Advice to a young catechumen: God bless you and persevere in your catechesis, which is forming your mind by disciplining all your thoughts and actions so that the ultimate presentation of them is in the greatest service to the Kingdom. Remember, the devil loves chaos. God is a God of order. All the ecstasies occur when believers follow the faith to its fullest.

A faithful echoing, a uniform teaching of the Faith is protection against the devil. The devil loves chaos. God is a God of order.

Chapter Ten

THE GOALIE

There is always a certain amount of tension as skaters try out for hockey teams. Will I make the team? What will my position be? Will it be a traveling team? Will I be with my best friends?

But there is one question in hockey that is a bit different from any other. When a family introduces a child to the ice, lurking somewhere is the question weighing most heavily on hockey parents, —"Will my child be a goalie?"

Parents react differently. Some hope that their child will become a goalie; perhaps even continuing a family tradition. Other parents are open to the possibility of a child's being a goalie, but it won't be something that they push, and some may secretly hope against it. There are those parents, however, who are vocal in their opposition to the goalie position. Oh, they are not opposed to the position *itself*, but they are opposed to the position for *their* children.

What is it about goalies? The cost. The goalie has by far the most expensive equipment and this expense falls on the family. Even if they buy used equipment, families will spend more on outfitting a goalie than for any other position on the team. Then there are growth spurts to contend with. A three-inch summer growth spurt can send a family into financial turmoil. New gloves, skates, and all-new pads become necessary. The mask and helmet might be okay for another year, but if there are new team colors that goalie may want the mask air-brushed accordingly.

The good thing about playing goalie is that goalies get the most ice time. Of course, that's true if your child is the *first string* goalie. Unfortunately, the *second string* goalie gets all of the expense and nearly none of the playing time, making the parents of the second string goalie perhaps the most dedicated in hockey. They keep the same commitments kept by every other family, their goalie is absolutely necessary to the team, and yet they may see their child take the ice just a few times during the season. Only the most generous families provide a goalie—especially a second string goalie.

The expense can be overwhelming. But it's not hard to imagine that a child who shows promise as a goalie can be supported; the family and even the community will contribute. Perhaps the family will have to make greater sacrifices; Grandma and Grandpa may even chip in. The community may rally to get used equipment and to reduce expenses, like sharing a room at the next out of town tournament.

The community understands the need for goalies. They know that providing a goalie is an exceptional gift of generosity. They realize that if a child is called to be a goalie, then that child should be given the opportunity. The community does what it can to support the vocation of goalie. It knows that hockey can't be hockey without a goalie. And that one goalie is not enough; there must be two.

Once I witnessed a particular youth hockey game where there was a goalie shortage; due to illness the opposing team didn't have a goalie. For the game to take place, our team had to loan a goalie to the other. Without the loan, the opposing team would have had to forfeit, sending our team forward in the tournament. But our skaters, aware that there is no glory in a forfeit, came to play; better to loan the goalie and take a chance of losing, than to leave the ice with a hollow victory. I have no recollection of who won the game, but I do remember the second string goalie fought with all his heart for the other team, and spectators sitting in the bleachers witnessed an amazing act of sportsmanship.

Imagine a skater with talent for the goalie position, yet the family refusing to let the child be a goalie. Imagine the community reaching out to the family; imagine the *call* from the community to the family: "You must allow the child to at least try."

In the early years skaters often begin as goalies but find they are not suited to the work. But they were *open* to the possibility. Rarely is it "once a goalie, always a goalie". In hockey, there are late vocations with boys and girls who begin as skaters and find their true position as goalies.

A hockey team, if it is to be a hockey team, must have a goalie. But there cannot be a team composed only of goalies. There must also be skaters. Many more hockey players are called to be skaters than goalies. The team must have both.

As a community, we support goalies and skaters. We do not begrudge a team its goalie. Neither do we expect that each child must be a goalie. The team is balanced when it contains two goalies and many skaters. No one begrudges the team a second goalie. And, if there is a goalie shortage, a goalie can help the opposing team.

+

When you are a faithful Catholic, the word gets out. From time to time, you are just an oddity, but at other times, a possible resource. A coworker came to me and complained of the new priest that was coming to her parish as pastor. She was upset about what she had heard of him and how, "if the Church would take care of the priest shortage," her parish wouldn't have to put up with priests like him. She told me of his *problems*. Ah, his *problem* is being faithful to the Magisterium. She pushed me, "What should we do; there *must* be something we can do!"

You're right; the Church should do something about the priest shortage. You, as a member of the Church, ought to take special care to do something about it. Why not teach a religious education class and create a special focus to make the children aware of vocations to the priesthood and religious life? And, once you marry your fiancé, be open to children—be *very* open to children.

We spoke further about the priest shortage. "Are you willing to give a child to the priesthood or to religious life?" She had never considered it. "Raise your children to be open to the vocation; this will precipitate the end of the crisis."

Could she imagine that this might be more effective than to attack the man who had been sent to her parish; a man who had given years of his life in service to the Church; a man who, from what was said, would be receiving anything but a warm welcome? If you are concerned, *do* something about it. Attacking and ostracizing priests is not doing anything except exacerbating the problem.

My coworker left a bit bewildered. Her question had been answered, but it wasn't the answer she had envisioned. *She* was to be the answer to the seeming problem. How very bewildering—what an amazing commission.

✝

My coworker married the man with whom she was living. Has she enrolled her children in hockey? Well, this is Minnesota and the odds are that they play hockey. Have any of her children become goalies? Hard to say, except that they were probably raised open to the possibility of becoming goalies.

In hockey, we may hear children say, "I could never be a goalie." The usual response is that they don't know until they have tried it.

Did my coworker and her husband raise their children open to vocations? Perhaps, but more likely not. In the Faith, we often hear children speak about not wanting to be called to a vocation. And, we hear of parents confirming them in this.

If God gives you a vocation, He will give you a peace and joy with which to enter a vocation. A friend once said that her grade school daughter was very nervous about being called to a vocation. She didn't need to decide now, the mother said, but remain open. "And besides, God may not be calling you; He may be calling someone through you. Your openness may be the way God reaches your friend. Now allow yourself to be open so He can do His work." What sage advice. Be open. God will do His work. Don't restrict God and the opportunities He may bring into your life.

Everyone agrees that there is a vocations shortage, but often we are uninterested in raising children open to a vocation. What a shame for the children. What a shame for the Church.

Be open: your child might be called to be a goalie or might not be. If our children are called to be goalies, the community is willing to rally around to support those vocations.

Be open: your child might be called to a religious vocation or might not be. If our children are called to religious vocations, the community will rally around to support those vocations.

Be open: let God do His work. Your imagination is not larger than God's omniscience. You may not be able to imagine the vocation, but God's knowledge is unlimited. Not everyone will become a priest or enter the religious life, but the Church *needs* these vocations. Not everyone will be called to the married life, but the Church *needs* married couples. Not everyone will be called to the single life, but the Church *needs* single people.

Be open and let God do His work.

Chapter Eleven

THE COMMISSIONER

The parents were enjoying some fellowship time before the game. There were a number of conversations taking place, covering things like the latest deal on skate sharpening to the new restaurant down the street and whether or not it is overpriced. Just minutes before the game Jack Anderson joined the group. One of the dads asked, "Hey, Jack, where've you been? Were you keeping warm in the car or something?"

"Nope, just drove up."

"What about Brittany, who brought her?"

"She just got here with me; she's getting dressed right now and should be on the ice in a minute or two."

"Wow, what a drag to be late. Now she can't play."

"No, she'll still be on the starting line."

Confused, the other dad asked Jack, "What are you talking about, she needed to be here an hour ago in order to play."

With a sort of swagger in his voice, Jack answered, "No, she'll be starting; I'm close personal friends with the commissioner."

Suddenly, all the other conversations stopped. Every parent was looking at Jack with that sort of he-can't-be-serious look.

Breaking the stunned silence, another dad spoke for everyone when he said, "*You can't be serious.* The rule is that the kids need to be here 45 minutes early, knowing, of course, that the kids like to have their own fellowship time 15 minutes before that. So all the kids need to be here an hour early."

Still with his vocal swagger, Jack said, "Yeah, I know the rules. But I think what you are all missing is the fact that I am close personal friends with the commissioner. Brittany will be on the starting line." Then, as if he were unaware of the bomb he just dropped, he asked, "Hey, anyone want some hot chocolate? My wife sent a thermos."

+

Wow! Imagine the reaction and general buzz among the other parents. How exactly does it follow that you can come late to the game and still play if you are close personal friends with the commissioner? The rules are the rules and nowhere in the rules is a provision made for close personal friends of the commissioner.

You can imagine a particular parent, who has bitten his tongue for long enough, finally bursting and saying, "Close personal friends? I don't break the rules of hockey and the Commissioner is a close personal friend of mine. In fact, He is such a close personal friend that I just had a Meal with Him on Sunday!"

I just had a Meal with Him on Sunday. We can pause a minute here so everyone is right with me—I just had a *Meal* with *Him* on *Sunday*.

The rules are the rules and the commissioner made them. In hockey, if a family is such close personal friends with the commissioner, it is probably more likely that they would abide by the rules, not wanting to exploit their friendship with him. Instead, they would respect him and his friendship. They would likely do everything by the book so no one would think the family was using their friendship, thereby causing scandal. Instead, the family would want to be beyond reproach.

Imagine how disrespectful it would seem to others as they observed the family exploiting the friendship. If the family were such close personal friends with the commissioner, all the more reason to keep his rules. And if the family were such close personal friends, how much more insulting to the commissioner when his close personal friends break the rules. Does his friendship mean nothing or is it just a relationship of convenience and exploitation?

The commissioner didn't make the rules just to make rules; he made the rules for *hockey*, for *all* the skaters. When the rules are followed, the greatness of hockey can be experienced. When the rules are discarded, even if just by his close personal friends, hockey is degraded. It becomes unsafe; it becomes chaos. Eventually it is not even hockey any more. Hockey has died. But, hockey is for life.

The rules are there not as traps, not as an obstacle course, not as a maze. No, the rules are there for life. The rules give very clear indications of what can and cannot be done, but there is tremendous freedom within the rules of hockey. Freedom is lost when the rules are broken.

I just had a Meal with Him on Sunday. Jesus has given us the rules and He gave us the Church to safeguard the rules and articulate them over time. We should each have a close personal friendship with Jesus. But this friendship is not a free pass for breaking, or even bending the rules.

"He won't really mind if I (fill-in-the-blank-with-your-favorite-sin)."

Yes, He will. And He will also mind the scandal that it causes when a close personal friend exploits His friendship.

Jesus is not a Man who wasted words; He *is* the Word. He gave us the rules, the Deposit of Faith, and a Church to safeguard it. The Church is His Bride; He loves Her. His love was the love of self-sacrifice, not of exploitation. When we take advantage of our close personal friendship with Christ, we exploit that friendship. When the rules are discarded, even if by His close personal friends, the Faith is degraded. Its status becomes precarious and chaotic. Eventually it is not even the Faith anymore. The Faith has died. But the Faith is for *life.*

If we claim such a close personal friendship with Christ, then all the more reason to respect His rules. If, however, in light of our close personal friendship with Christ, we break the rules—or only *bend* the rules, the offense is that much more grave. A friendship with the Commissioner ought to be one of mutual respect, mutual sacrifice, and never a relationship of exploitation.

Imagine how disappointed we are when our friends let us down or exploit our friendship for personal gain. It causes a wound to the friendship. Then imagine the feeling of love and pride when your friend acts out of love for you, sacrificing for you, doing what is right. The friendship is intensified; it has become deeper.

If someone were to say, "He is a close personal friend with the Commissioner," the answer should not be a disdainful and jealous, "It shows." Instead the answer should be said with a certain awe and wonder, "It shows!" If you are close personal friends with the Commissioner, let it show. Act out of love for Christ, sacrifice for him, do what is right, follow His rules. Let His face brighten with a proud love for you. When you meet Him face to face, may He say, "Ah, my close personal friend, I've been waiting for you. There is a place prepared for you!"

Chapter Twelve

CROSS CHECKING

Emily is a good skater, but not a great skater. She has done quite well and made the ninth grade junior varsity team, but it is nearly certain that she will not make the varsity team for the rest of her time in high school. The school is large and the competition very tough, so ninth grade will most likely be the last year of formal instruction in hockey for Emily.

With this in mind, it is still the wish of everyone, her parents, coaches, and teammates, that she will continue to participate in hockey. The hope is that she continues to attend high school hockey games, and that one day she will study at a college with a hockey team, enjoying those games as well. Emily may even join high school and college intramural teams, and maybe a city league after college.

It would be great if Emily met a nice young man from a hockey family, possibly a skater himself. It would be great if they married, possibly having hockey sticks raised on either side of the aisle as they left the church. (Wait—that's going a bit too far. Don't even mention this to your priest.) But they could one day have little skaters of their own. Emily and her future husband might even coach, especially in the early years when good volunteers are so very important.

Even though this year might be the last formal opportunity that Emily will have to play hockey, there is hope that she will remain faithful. Her ninth grade coaches are aware of the spot they are in with

Emily and other skaters like her. They are the last disciples who may ever teach her. This is quite a responsibility and it is not lost on them.

Taking into account their grave responsibility, and aware that this will most likely be the last point of contact between Emily and the formal catechesis of hockey, the disciples have come up with a plan. It's their best plan, the one they use with everyone in her situation, the plan to keep her faithful. They speak of it almost in a whisper because of its importance.

"Let's not tell her about cross checking!"

"What? Let's not tell her about cross checking? Are you crazy? Isn't cross checking against the rules? How is Emily to remain faithful to hockey when she is not fully catechized?"

"Well, we didn't want to tell her about cross checking because it might turn her off, she might leave hockey if we tell her *that*. We just want to make this time as comfortable for Emily as possible so she doesn't leave hockey."

"Yes, but it's against the rules! I mean, in cross checking you are shoving the handle of the stick into the opponent while you are holding the stick in both hands. How exactly does that fit into the rules?"

"Well, technically, it doesn't. But it's the sort of thing that can really alienate kids at this age."

"Yes, but doesn't not telling Emily about cross checking put her in danger of incurring penalties? Couldn't her lack of knowledge actually *hurt* her, not to mention hurting other skaters?"

"Well, it really depends on what you call a penalty. It's not a penalty if you don't get caught. And as for *hurting*, well, Emily is a careful skater; it really shouldn't matter."

✝

Wow! This would *never* happen in hockey!

The catechesis of hockey applies across the board to all skaters according to their age level and ability. In hockey, we don't hold back potentially uncomfortable teachings in order to *protect* the skaters. In fact, in hockey there are no uncomfortable teachings. Why? Because everyone is fully catechized to their age level. Nothing is left unsaid. The disciples of hockey are not embarrassed by the teachings, nor do they dissent from the teachings. The rules are the rules, there are *full* reasons behind the rules, and disciples have taken the time to learn those reasons themselves.

Let's revisit the use of helmets. When five- or six-year-old children first join a team, they are sent to the ice with helmets. What do they know of the reason for wearing helmets? They have seen everyone using a helmet and have little curiosity regarding the piece of hard plastic on their heads. If they do ask why, parents and coaches probably answer in the same way, "It's part of the uniform, kid."

As skaters grow, however, perhaps they begin to be curious about the protection the helmet offers. Why is the plastic formed in the manner it is? Why the interior pads? Why the plastic over the face? It would be easy to imagine a particularly curious skater who later becomes an engineer trying to improve upon the helmet.

The catechesis about the helmet is age appropriate. It begins with "it's part of the uniform" and may end in the subtle nuances of pressure, protection, lightness, durability, and comfort. A skater is catechized according to age level and ability.

Let's look at another example: body checking into the boards, which is different than cross checking. Body checking is usually just called checking, and has to do with using angles and the boards to cause a collision with the puck carrier in an attempt to free the puck from the opponent. Checking someone into the boards is a legal part of hockey, but not at five years of age.

The five-year-olds are just learning how to stand on their skates. They may be still watching their feet as they skate. There is a good chance that a number of five-year-old skaters have no idea where the puck is at any given time; they may have been assigned positions, but they are more likely to be skating in a large clump than to be in their respective positions.

If a five-year-old were to ask about checking, it is doubtful the coach would explain that skaters must learn to keep their heads up as they near the boards in case someone were to check them, protecting the neck and head and improving the odds against damage to the brain and spinal cord. More likely, the coach tells these young skaters that checking is against the rules and not to do it.

But there is a time when checking is allowed in hockey; the usual age is eleven- or twelve-years-old. There may be some discussion as to whether this is the right age, but there is no discussion that skaters, at the appropriate time, must be taught how to check, how to take a check, and how to protect themselves as they near the boards in order not to be hurt by a check. Checking is a part of hockey, at the appropriate age.

The practice of checking does carry some debate. Should skaters be allowed to check at a younger age or should they be older? Should particular leagues allow checking or not? The disciples have some heated opinions. Checking may be considered a *difficult* teaching of hockey, but it is a teaching all the same.

When it is appropriate, checking is taught in hockey. Body checking is substantially different from cross checking, or even checking from behind. Body checking is allowed at a certain age. Cross checking and checking from behind, because of their grave danger to skaters, are never allowed. The nuances in teaching are important parts of the teaching, and these teachings are given to skaters at the appropriate ages.

+

We would never hold back the appropriate hockey catechesis from Emily, especially if it were our last opportunity to catechize her in hockey.

Imagine the uproar in hockey if we kept the rules of the game from our children. Yet, constantly we hear well-meaning parents and catechists of all sorts saying that we do our children a favor by keeping the teaching of the rules of the Church from them. The hope is that this will keep them faithful, yet it almost never works.

Take for example, the Church's teaching on abortion. Certainly, there are parishes and Catholic schools that boldly teach against abortion. In many places, however, the teaching on abortion is considered too controversial to be met head-on.

Much formal Catholic teaching with children begins when they are five- or six-years-old in Catholic kindergartens or after-school faith formation programs. The pro-life teaching begins simply, with the respect and love due even to the very youngest of human beings. Because of the child's tender age, it is not appropriate to delve into the nitty-gritty of the Church's teaching on abortion. As children mature they are given more information. Perhaps they make blankets and collect money for life care centers. In science classes they may begin to understand the stages of life of the unborn baby. And then, at an appropriate time, they are taught about the evil of abortion.

It often seems the timing of the deeper understanding of abortion coincides with Confirmation classes and the approaching end of the high school years. Catechists know this may be the last opportunity for these students to receive *formal Catholic teaching.* Teachers are also aware that the Church's stance against abortion may not be what the student has learned at home. And, what the world teaches the student is the antithesis of what the Church teaches. The use of simple sound bites to teach the truth is ineffective. In short, teaching the truth is time consuming, controversial, and not for ninnies.

The Catholic Church calls *all* teachers to teach the truth. Bishops, priests, catechists, parents, doctors, scientists—everyone who teaches our children is charged with teaching them the truth, in season and out of season. But we teachers often cower. It was fine to teach them about loving babies, but to really speak out about abortion can be difficult. We use the excuse that it is better not to confront our children with the difficult teachings, in the hope that this will help them to remain faithful throughout their lives.

However, a quick survey of young adults will show you that the poorly catechized rarely remain faithful. When catechists teach only the doctrines that we are "comfortable" with, the Catholic religion seems like any other religion. Which makes the exodus that much easier for those raised with only a warm and fuzzy faith.

Why are there difficult teachings in the Church? Because we refuse to look at them. Nothing is uncomfortable when we teach it at the appropriate time, and when we give it the appropriate weight. These truths are utterly logical and stack neatly atop of teachings that students already have. Our children possess a surprising ability to understand Catholic catechism. When we don't offer them the meat and potatoes of the Faith they become bored and disenfranchised. But when a teacher digs into a teaching, there is nothing more wonderful than to see the growing light in the eyes of the students. It's a satisfying experience for both.

✝

One of the most amazing gifts I have ever been given was the opportunity to teach RCIA classes (The Rite of Christian Initiation for Adults). It was a great joy to be with adults about to be confirmed and their sponsors. Many sponsors informed me that they had received twelve years of Catholic education, or had participated in nine years of religious education, or something along those lines. They were a little stunned to learn they were required to attend classes each week with the confirmands. Yet often it was the sponsors who commented, "I never knew that! How come no one ever told me that?" Their encounter with the depth of Catholic teaching was a shock to them. Sometimes these sponsors were the only Catholics that the confirmands knew. Sometimes sponsors weren't entirely faithful until the confirmand called them to faithfulness by requesting the favor of their sponsorship.

There was a questioning disappointment in their voices. "How come no one ever told me that?"

They had believed many teachings didn't matter, or had mattered only a long time ago, and ranged from the simple—"Really, we have to fast for an hour before Communion?"—to things as profound as the Church's stance on abortion.

"How come no one ever told me that?"

Perhaps no one told you in order to prevent hurt feelings, to keep you faithful, to help you, to be *pastoral*—but the disappointment in their voices betrayed the fact that they never felt protected by not knowing, they hadn't been more faithful because of not knowing, they had never been helped by not knowing. It had been anything *but* pastoral to keep them uncatechized. Their disappointment was the disappointment of *years* lost, and at times even of grave woundedness.

Their surprise was nearly always followed by a simple observation: "If the Church would just let people know that this is the reason, then people could understand the teaching on (fill-in-the-blank)."

Is there a teaching you are keeping from your child? It is time to seek out the answers, and the manner in which to teach it. At the appropriate age, we must catechize our children *fully*.

Chapter Thirteen

THE UNIFORM

There is nearly nothing more majestic than seeing your team, let's say the University of Minnesota Golden Gophers, taking the ice in their uniforms. Something about it gets the heart pumping. There is an eternal hope for a great game and an eventual victory.

It is the same with any hockey team. The five-year-olds, the pros, the teenagers—there is a particular, unexplainable beauty in seeing the team in uniform as they take the ice for the first time. So imagine the surprise to everyone around if one skater was not in uniform, but instead wearing flip-flops, shorts, and a tank top. We might wonder whether the kid had lost a bet or was doing it on a dare. But no one would expect anyone to skate—or rather slide—in flip-flops, shorts, and a tank top.

Why not? Simply, stepping out onto the ice in that attire would be unsafe. Of course it would be unsafe for the skater, but perhaps even more so for the other skaters. If somehow this skater were allowed on the ice—perhaps because the non-uniform idea was an act of free will, and no one would want to squash a child's free will—appearing on the ice in flip-flops, shorts, and a tank top not only hampers the skater's team, but the opposing team as well. A normal game of hockey suddenly becomes inordinately dangerous.

Let's name the scantily clad skater Alex. The danger to him seems obvious. In a particular manner both teams must bear Alex in mind.

They do not want to skate too near, as they may run over his toes with their own skates. His fellow skaters can no longer shoot or pass the puck in his direction as it could hit a shin, or an arm, or the jaw, or somewhere. It has become morally impermissible to check him into the boards because of the likelihood of grave harm.

There are other dangers. In their concern to avoid injuring Alex, skaters are paying less attention to the game at hand. Distracted skating is unsafe skating, leaving those skaters open to injury. Alex's desire to play hockey unencumbered by his uniform has taken freedom away from the team, the body of which he is a part, as the team no longer has the ability to skate as it should.

It is easy to imagine that if this were allowed to happen at a youth hockey game, parents and skaters would react sharply. Perhaps some parents would pull their own children from the ice and go home. Others might insist their children remain on the bench were Alex allowed to skate. These children, unable to take part in the game because of the danger, would now be able to participate only passively from the bench, not actively on the ice. Still others might allow their children to skate, provided they pay close attention to avoid harming him.

However parents chose to handle the problem, skaters would be called upon to do one thing: protect Alex. It's their responsibility as members of the team. But somewhere on a sheet of ice, in some arena, there may be a skater who doesn't heed the warning of parents, or who wasn't warned at all, and who now sees it as a personal mission to do bodily harm to Alex. It certainly isn't right, but it's not hard to imagine.

Organized hockey calls for a uniform. The team's name and colors lend themselves to the majesty of the game. But these are only decorations to the uniform. The "nuts and bolts" of the uniform are for the protection of skaters; the pads, the helmet, the gloves, and the boot of the skate are all made in a manner that protects the skater. If a player steps onto the ice out of uniform, there is a very real danger present not only to that skater but also to the body that is the team. Everything about the uniform is appropriate to hockey; it is about the safety of the team. Everything about the uniform is ordered toward the preservation of life.

Basketball calls for a uniform. Football calls for a uniform. Soccer calls for a uniform. Even ballet calls for a sort of uniform. Every team has an *appropriate* uniform. There is a particular uniform in everyday life called modesty in dress. When we are "out of uniform," the team is less free. When our children are out of uniform in everyday life, if they are not dressed modestly and appropriately for a given activity, they take freedom from the team and they shirk their responsibility to the team.

There may be those who choose not to be in the presence of your immodestly and inappropriately dressed child. Others may choose to be near but not directly to accompany your child. There may be others who will maintain custody of the eyes, remaining with your child, but not ogling them. But one day, somewhere, sometime, there may be someone who makes it a personal mission to harm your child because your child is out of the uniform that goes by the name of modest dress. It certainly doesn't make it right, but it is far too easy to imagine.

There is a uniform in hockey, and parents and coaches make certain the skaters are in uniform. They are expected to make corrections as needed. It is the scantily clad skater who would be seen as bold for being out of uniform.

There is a uniform in everyday life: modest dress. Yet, if someone is out of uniform, it is seen as *intolerant* to offer correction. Parents, teachers, and peers are criticized for addressing immodesty. What is modesty? Modesty has to do with what is appropriate to the situation. A basketball player doesn't wear football cleats; that would be unsafe. A football player doesn't wear a basketball uniform; that would be unsafe. Protecting athletes is a given, and protecting our children should receive the same consideration.

Imagine Alex or the basketball player in football cleats. Would we ever be able to look at Alex and appreciate his dignity as a skater? Would we ever be able to look at the basketball player wearing football cleats and be able to appreciate his dignity as a basketball player? We may not be able to take our eyes off them, but that is probably because of our concern for them or our shock *for* them.

When a child is dressed as a skater, we *see* the child as a skater. When we view a scantily clad skater, we see the act of free will as immaturity, we see the decision-making abilities as malformed, and we may possibly even see the skater as a *fool*. It's the same for the basketball player in football cleats. No one would recognize his dignity as a player. Instead, the murmur may be, "What does that idiot think he is doing!" We would be utterly shocked if someone were allowed on the ice or the parquet without the proper uniform. "Why won't someone stop this? It is dangerous for everyone!"

+

"Wait a minute! Don't think that I can't read between the lines. You're saying that I can't be a good Catholic unless I cover every inch of my body."

"Nope, that's not what I'm saying."

"Yes, it is. And I'm here to tell you that you are wrong and I take offense at your implications. It doesn't matter how I'm dressed, I can still pray!"

"I completely agree, you can pray no matter how you are dressed. Even if you are undressed you should still be able to pray. Take for example when you are in the shower in the morning, it's probably not a bad time to ask God what He would like of you that day. It's not a bad time to tell Him that you will spend the day serving Him. Then later when you are in your robe and drying your hair, it's not a bad idea to ask Him to remember your friend who is sick, or your child who has a test in school, or for the repose of the soul of your uncle. You are completely right, you can pray no matter how you are dressed."

"Now you sound funny, like you are trying to twist my words."

"No, I'm agreeing with you. You can pray no matter how you

are dressed. However, the problem with modesty comes as other people are added into the scene. Even in families, there is a different level of modesty with a spouse than with children. Further, there is a different level of modesty with the repairman sent to fix the squeaky dryer than with the rest of the family. As other people are added to your situation, your understanding of modesty changes."

Remember the boy on the sheet of ice with skates, a stick, a crushed can for a puck and a few twigs marking off the goal? He can play hockey without all the pads and still remain safe. It's when others are added to the game; as the number of players increases, the padding seems to increase as well. Soon, there are two teams in an arena, the intensity of the skating has increased, they are in the midst of a game; all the skaters must now be in the full hockey uniform. That first boy can play hockey just the way he is, alone. It's just that as the situation changes, what is appropriate changes also.

✝

So now we enter a dangerous territory. What *exactly* can we wear? Well, let me answer this in a few ways.

Once, at Mass, I saw a teenaged boy in a t-shirt that said, "No Mercy" in words that nearly covered the back of the shirt. I wondered where we would be if Jesus had worn such a garment. The t-shirt was inappropriate even though it wasn't exactly *immodest*. Nevertheless, it was shocking and disrespectful. Although I tried to look away, I found myself continually looking at him, distracted from the prayer of the Mass.

One summer day I was at a Mass where a few babies were to be baptized. When one of the mothers stood up, I was taken aback by how little she was wearing. Her dress was quite short and had tiny spaghetti straps. The amount of skin she was displaying was distracting, even *continually* distracting. Attempting to concentrate on the baptism was no help; she was holding the baby! Even closing my eyes seemed useless, as I couldn't "un-see" her unfortunate choice of clothing. Later that morning, I accompanied friends to their country club for brunch. As we sat eating, a family came in with a tiny baby. It was the same family that I had seen in church. The mother was wearing the same thing, but now the dress was accompanied by a sweater. The country club had a dress code that included no bare shoulders. Lest you think it had to do with the air-conditioning, the church was just as chilly. I found it odd that she had no qualms about appearing scantily clad in church, yet took care to cover up at the country club.

A student once asked me what the problem was with having bare shoulders in church, seeing as how bare shoulders are not sexual. Another student asked a similar question about a bare midriff. They both had arguments that went something like this: a bare shoulder is the same as a bare elbow is the same as a bare wrist is the same as a bare hand. It's not like I'm showing "anything."

It certainly is a fine argument, until you consider how comfortable you are when a stranger touches you on your bare shoulders or midriff. "If they really are the same as your bare hand, why would it matter if instead of shaking your hand, a stranger touched your shoulders or stomach?" Both students recoiled. I asked them, "What's different? Because something *is* different." Neither of them had an answer—they only had their instinctive reactions.

What is different? Familiarity—even a sort of intimacy. A stranger does not enjoy a familiarity with you, therefore he should not touch you in a familiar way. The closer to the trunk of the body, the more sacred that part of the body is. Obviously, this has different boundaries for boys and girls.

But it doesn't seem that I've answered the question, "What *exactly* can we wear?" In fact, I don't really intend to answer this question, except in one situation: what to wear in church.

Being in church, and especially being at Mass, calls for wearing a uniform. One simple rule is: except for the very young, everyone should have his or her shoulders and knees covered in church, especially at Mass.

Yes, I can hear the counter-arguments already. But we have already established the intimacy of the body, being more intimate the nearer the trunk of the body. There is nothing more intimate than the Mass—but it is intimate in a completely different manner. Out of respect for those around you, take care and dress appropriately at Mass. *You* do not have to look at yourself during Mass, but everyone else must.

The Mass is the Perfect Prayer. Everyone has distractions at prayer, and we will all face distractions at Mass, usually from our own thoughts. We are a part of the Mystical Body and we must care for the other members in the Body. Immodesty is a distraction and it diminishes the freedom of Christ's Mystical Body to pray without distraction.

The first skater on the sheet of ice appropriately skates without pads when he is alone. However, when he is in the midst of a game with other skaters, additional care is shown as he dons his pads, thereby respecting his own dignity and that of the other skaters. Our bodies speak, and we must be aware of what they are saying to others. The scantily clad skater tells the other skaters that he cares nothing for their freedom. Immodesty says the same to those around us.

We, too, must recognize our own dignity and that of the members of the Mystical Body. Modesty in dress is one of the ways in which we do so. By being modest, a person shows that he or she understands that he or she is worth more than to be an object that attracts stares; he or she is worth more than to be an object of mere gawking. Being modest is a sign of maturity and restraint; proper decision-making takes into account the full situation, not just self-centered impulses. Modesty indicates a recognition of one's own dignity, the recognition that if one is ever to be taken for a fool, it should be as a fool for Christ, not a fool for fashion.

Chapter Fourteen

WWJGD

Minnesota *is* the State of Hockey, but that's not all we have. Minnesota is also the home of the winningest college football coach of all time, Coach John Gagliardi. With nearly seventy years of coaching under his belt from high school to college level, he is a Minnesota state institution and a treasure. After completing his sixtieth year of coaching the St. John Johnnies, Gagliardi announced his retirement.

It happens that my friends have a son who played for Gagliardi. Like all parents who had sons playing for Gagliardi, my friends were over the moon. This was a dream not just for their son, but also for their family, and even for their friends. We all knew little David, and now he would be playing for the Johnnies!

David's parents dropped him off at St. John's University in early August. The parents left in a daze on this momentous day. A week passed before his parents could speak to David. They had only one question, and couldn't wait to hear the answer from their son, but more about that later. In the meantime, David began practice. It was unlike any other football practice he had attended. John Gagliardi's manner of coaching was markedly different from anything he had previously encountered, including the mandate to call him John and not Coach.

In high school, David had been the big man on campus and a star football player; it only made sense that he would be recruited by the Johnnies. Now at practice for college football, David experienced

a revelation. He was no longer the best on the field. He discovered
that he might not be starting as a freshman and possibly not attend
all the travel games.

The first week had passed. His parents were in a heightened state
all week, waiting to have their one question answered. They were
both on the phone when they were finally able to ask. Even though
they had anticipated the answer all week, they still breathlessly asked,
"How do you like John Gagliardi?"

With a week of practice under his belt, David was able to syn-
thesize his answer. "He's an idiot!"

Ah—the wounded pride of an 18-year-old: "He's an idiot!" It's
beautiful in a way. Immediately we can all recall our own wounded
pride as teenagers. Each one of us has been there, and David's dec-
laration is received with a gentle chortle and a knowing nod. "Yes,
David, we're just sure that John Gagliardi, the winningest college
football coach of all time, is an idiot." Wounded pride is just fantastic.

If I were looking for an opinion on football and had to choose
between John Gagliardi and David, I would go with John Gagliardi
every single time. Even if the question were, "What is the typical
18-year-old football player thinking these days?" John's would be
the desired answer. Surely he understands the 18-year-old football
player brain more than *anyone,* including 18-year-old football
players! No matter what, John is the go-to on football. There is just
no arguing with his record: winningest college football coach of all
time; 69 years of coaching; 64 years of college football coaching;
the first active coach inducted into the college football hall of fame;
four national championship teams; 30 conference titles; his 1993
team scored a season *average* of 61.5 points *per game.* There have
been 25,000 college football coaches in the United States and only
two have won over 400 games; John won 489.[3] Yes, John Gagliardi
is the man to see for *any* football answers.

---

[3] St. John's University, "John Gagliardi: The Winningest Coach in College Football History"
<http://www.gojohnnies.com/staff.aspx?staff=9&path=football>

In football my motto is WWJGD—What Would John Gagliardi Do?

As it turns out David played four years of football with John. However, it didn't take four years for David to change his mind about John; that happened within the second week of his freshman football camp with the Johnnies. What changed? David became docile to the seemingly nonsensical teaching of John Gagliardi.

Why is John's teaching seemingly nonsensical? John has a coaching technique referred to as "Winning with No." Among other *no's*, John does not use blocking sleds or dummies in practice; there are no whistles; there is no tackling in practice; practice is no longer than 90 minutes; there are no compulsory weightlifting programs; there are no athletic scholarships offered; and, as mentioned before, no one calls him Coach, his team calls him John.[4]

On paper, John's techniques don't make much sense and with no scholarships offered, it's a wonder he has any players. Or is it? Players like David, who have completed four years of football with John and have been docile to his teachings, leave with the understanding that he taught them much more than football. John taught them life lessons that they applied to every area of their lives. John Gagliardi taught them how to be *men*. Scholarships weren't the incentive; playing for John was.

Now and again, there is a Church teaching that to some might seem as ridiculous as John Gagliardi's teaching methods. Now and again, when asked what we think of the Church's teachings on a particular thing, we might be tempted to proclaim, "This is idiotic!"

David had about 13 years of football experience under his belt. From a young boy on, he was a gifted football player. He had been the big man on campus for four years of high school. Football was

---
[4] Frank Rajkowski, *Gagliardi: Road to the Record* (St. Cloud, MN: St. Cloud Times, 2003) 10.

his life. He lived, breathed, slept, dreamed, and played football. Yet, John's teachings clanged against his ear; his methods of teaching were counter-cultural. So why did we chortle when David, no stranger to football, proclaimed John to be an idiot? With no disrespect to David, we recognized John as the expert and we recognized an 18-year-old with the clouded vision of wounded pride. Having been given the gift of just a few more years and a touch of wisdom, we knew that once David submitted to the teachings, he would come to understand John's greatness. We knew that the teachings were more than just about football. And we knew that David would come to love John's teachings, even reaching for them in all future endeavors and allowing them to change his life.

We have the same wounded pride. We have attended CCD and Catholic schools. We go to Mass and listen to the homilies. We have a Bible and a Catechism in our homes. We were married in the Church, our children were baptized in the Church, and we send them to CCD and Catholic schools. Surely, we have a certain expertise in Catholic teaching.

When given a choice, we will go with John Gagliardi over David every time when it comes to a question having to do with football. John's record just cannot be denied. When it comes to my four years of CCD and my eight years of Catholic schools by the time I left high school, regular Mass attendance and occasional Catholic Bible study, weighed against the 2000-year-old unbroken tradition established by Jesus Christ and maintained in the Church He established, we have to go with the Church *every time!*

David had temporarily placed himself above authority; it was his wounded pride speaking. Later, he realized that there was a lot more to John Gagliardi and his teachings, but this happened only after he became docile to them. He discovered the teachings were beautiful after he gave them a chance. He was surprised that these teachings were following him through life, becoming a part of each day. He was surprised when he came to love what he thought he never could. When we are tempted to declare the Church and Her teachings idiotic, remember David, the football player, and recognize our wounded pride. Pride caused the Fall.

The cure for our wounded pride is docility. Docility means being teachable. Beneath every difficult Catholic dogma or doctrine that might seem to ring untrue, there is a vast, beautiful teaching! If we allow ourselves, we may come to understand the teaching, we may come to see the beauty of the teaching, and the teaching may translate into every area of our lives.

When John Gagliardi recruited football players, he didn't ask them to leave their football brains at the door. If he wanted that, he would have recruited tennis players or stamp collectors. But John recruited football players, and he asked them to bring all they knew of football with them to the Johnnies. Then he called them to be docile to his teaching and to be formed by his teaching, thereby calling them to a higher standard of football.

It is the same in the Church. The Church does not ask you to leave your brain at the door; instead She calls you to engage your brain! Bring all that you know, be docile to the teachings, allow Her to form you, thereby calling you to higher things.

Often there are complaints that the teachings of the Church are only a list of things you cannot do. But no one complained about Gagliardi's list of *no's*. Instead, as radical as his teachings were, they were celebrated. With John at the helm, the Johnnies said *no* to a number of things that are normal for every other football team in the country. In football, Gagliardi stood virtually alone with his *no's*.

If John rejected things like blocking sleds and dummies, long practices, whistles, weight lifting programs, and scholarships, didn't he reject football? No, he embraced football. His list of *no's* allowed his team to say yes; to say *yes* to football. In saying *yes* to one thing, there is necessarily a rejection of something else. John didn't have his players just sitting around thinking about football; he had regimented practices that emphasized repetition and fundamentals.[5] He

---

[5] St. John's University, "John Gagliardi," <http://www.gojohnnies.com/staff.aspx?staff=9>..

knew what was needed to win and he distilled it and gave it to his players in a clear, straightforward manner. He rejected everything that kept his players from victory. The reason John's "Winning with No" was radical was that it was really not a list of *no's*, instead it was one great *yes* for victory.

The Church is the same. Her list of *no's*, or sins, is really one great *yes*, one Great Amen. Our yes is to Christ. In order to say "Amen" perfectly to Christ and His Church, we must necessarily say *no* to what is not of Him, namely sin. We will never be in *perfect* union with Christ, we will never *perfectly* have "put on Christ," unless and until we reject all sin.

Did John's teams say *yes* perfectly? No, even they fell at times. Is falling a reason to quit? No, John taught *beyond* the individual game. "My whole team, my whole years, I've never had goals, just great expectations."[6] No wonder John coached for nearly seventy years—he *expected* more. If Gagliardi were looking only to break records, he could have quit; many of his possibly unbreakable records were set years before his retirement. John and his teams *expected* greatness and lived to say *yes* to football another day.

Do the members of the Church say *yes* perfectly? No, the first Fall has caused many more falls. Is falling a reason to quit? No, the Church teaches *beyond* the Fall. The Church has great expectations for Her children. And even after our falls, we live to say *yes* to Christ once again.

John Gagliardi stood virtually alone in football with his list of *no's*. The Church stands alone in Her list of *no's*. John's list of *no's* made it possible to say *yes* perfectly to football. The Church's list of *no's* make it possible to say *yes* perfectly to Christ.

---

[6] Ibid

Chapter Fifteen

THE SLAP SHOT

My friend's son, Chris, was a talented young hockey player. He was probably twelve- or thirteen-years-old at the time, and one of the best on a team at the highest level of their age group. He played hockey from late summer to late spring; he took a break only to play summer baseball. While watching Chris play, it was easy to tell that he was a talented boy—but he was still a boy.

The University of Minnesota Gopher Hockey Team held a summer camp at which Chris was a participant. It happened that at the camp the Gopher players saw his talent as well. As a special project and in their spare time, the Gopher players took Chris under their collective wing and taught him the slap shot. For one week, he had his own slap shot mentors.

At the first regular game after the camp, it was as if someone different was living in his body. A boy had gone off to the Gopher camp, but they had sent a man back. The first time he had an opportunity, he used his newly acquired slap shot. It was blistering, absolutely breathtaking, and a collective gasp came from the crowd. The shot was so powerful that it almost seemed an optical illusion. But the slap shot came again and again. We had already seen it five times, and each time it was just as shocking. This boy had the power of a man. The slap shot had, at the same time, a beauty and a danger about it.

The boys on the team were talented skaters—but they were still boys. At one point, the puck was up against the boards. All the boys skated around it, trying to wrestle it away for their respective team. Only four skaters remained in position at the time: the two goalies, Chris at mid-ice, and his teammate to the right of the opposition's net. The puck was kicked out and it came to Chris.

He wound up; there was another gasp from the crowd. Two thoughts were simultaneously on everyone's mind: that scalding slap shot and the safety of the goalie. Chris wound up—and then the most extraordinary thing happened. He swept the puck easily to his teammate near the goal and the teammate tapped it into the goal.

There was the briefest moment of silence as we all tried to comprehend what we had just seen. This was followed by a sustained cheer, not just from our side, but also from the fans of the opposing team. We all knew that we had witnessed something extraordinary. Chris knew that he had the ability. But he knew something more, that glory for the team was more important than glory for self. He went for the sure thing, not the flashy thing. An unselfish act had brought him more glory than the slap shot could.

Over the years, I have often thought of this play. I had never witnessed anything like it before, and have never seen anything close to it since. Perhaps it was because I knew the story on and off the ice that made the play so amazing to me.

+

An opportunity presented itself to Chris—the Gopher Hockey Camp. His family saw the wisdom in sending him and committed to the camp. The money was found, the time was made, and the boy went off to a type of hockey *retreat*. It was a week-long event; all the boys attending stayed together in the dorms; they spent every waking moment on the ice. They skated from morning to evening; they lived, breathed, slept, dreamed, and played hockey. They were surrounded by great teachers, not just the Gopher players, but also the Gopher coaches. These coaches were like spiritual retreat masters.

The boys were novices coming to learn from the spiritual masters. They were asked to submit themselves to a week of *everything* hockey. During the week they were not taught how to ignore or overcome the rules; they were taught how to submit to and master the rules. They were expected to be docile to the teachings of the spiritual masters and to give them undivided attention. The boys gave themselves physically and spiritually to hockey.

When the Gopher players spotted the talent in my friend's son and offered to teach the slap shot to him in their spare time, he made a deeper commitment, foregoing his breaks. From what Chris said later, we discovered this intense slap shot mentoring was given only to him; he was the only skater ready for it. It was no surprise, then, that he would have something that nearly no other player at his level would have—the power of a man's slap shot. Perhaps he could not fully understand what he had been given, but he must have seen the difference in his power and that of his teammates. However, the boy was not shy about his talent. He didn't hide it in order to fit in, he now stood out in a crowd. He had a talent that had been nurtured deeply, and he used the gift that had been given to him in the proper place and time.

There had already been times in the game when he used his slap shot to no avail. He had not previously used it for a goal; he had not yet made a goal in the game. Perhaps a lesser player would have given up on the slap shot having seen no fruits. But this boy had trust in his talent, trust in his coaching, and trust in the truth: the slap shot is an effective tool in hockey.

Though others were not at his level, he was still on their team and he brought all of his talent to the ice. He did not *dumb down* his game. In fact, he was so aware of what he was there to do as a skater, he remained in position when nearly all other players were out of position to chase a wayward puck. He had the wherewithal to calmly stay in position instead of heading to the fray to seek to be the one to free the puck. In position, he waited for what was to come. And what came was an amazing opportunity.

There were only seconds between the puck being kicked away from the boards and the puck going into the goal. There was no time to map out a strategy. The opportunity was only available for a split second. What did the boy rely upon? Discipline. Where did he get it? Years of training, not just the training with the Gophers the week before. The training had been consistent, at times seemingly unending and pointless, and unbearably tedious. Conditioning was done over and over, drilling was done over and over, passing was done over and over. Every fiber of Chris was that of a hockey player, which included respect for the *rules* of hockey. When the opportunity came, he was able to react immediately and seize the opportunity.

The goal was to get the puck into the opponent's net. The opposing goalie had seen the boy's slap shot five previous times, but each time before the goalie had other defenders to help him. This time Chris wound up and the goalie knew that it was *mano a mano*. But the boy only *showed* the slap shot, he didn't *use* it.

Chris remembered his teammate was in position, in a great position to the right of the goal. He brought his stick forward to the puck and the years of passing drills bore fruit in that moment as he tapped the puck to his teammate and the teammate tapped it into the goal.

Perhaps the biggest surprise should not be that Chris had the talent, knowledge, and instincts to tap the puck to his teammate. It seems that the bigger surprise is the readiness of the teammate. He was the only other one in the arena prepared for the brilliant move of the boy at mid-ice.

I have already said that my friend's son was the most talented on the team and even more so after the Gopher hockey camp. The boy to the right of the goal was *not* the most talented; yet he was ready. How is it possible? He had been through the same conditioning and drilling and the general tedium of training. Training and conditioning is not just for the great skaters; it is for *each* skater. During the everyday ordinary training that goes on year after year the skaters learn the *rules* of hockey. No one would think to put an untrained skater on the ice during the game. His reactions haven't been honed, he has no *feel* for his teammates, he has no conditioning in order to maintain a high level of play; it might well be dangerous to put him on the ice under these conditions.

Back to the teammate to the side of the goal—he was the only one ready. He saw the slap-shot-wind-up but was ready for the tap. He *received* the tap and then gently tapped it into the goal. It was just a flick of the wrist; so soft and so unexpected. This skater was just as ready for the opportunity; the opportunity that could have been lost with even a moment's hesitation.

The aim was a goal for the team, not a goal for self-glory. The opportunity was brief and fleeting. A lesser skater may have seen the opportunity as a wide open shot and taken it himself, taking his chances with the goalie. But Chris had talent beyond his age, and he had a *humility* as well. Chances are that he could have made the shot himself, but the chances were so much greater that the goal could be made by the unexpected teammate closer to the net. The goal was the goal, not glory for self. The certain path was through the teammate.

And what happened when the goal was made? The crowd went wild. But on the ice there was a celebration as well. Chris was already skating toward his teammate to celebrate. The rest of the team followed; the celebration was on as the teammates hugged and hollered and jumped on each other. It was a moment of utter joy. The *team* celebrated their good fortune. The glory was for the team, but the team instinctively shared the glory with the individuals.

The spectators were stunned by the simple elegance of the play. The talent of my friend's son was already remarkable; and now our estimation of him had grown immensely. His greatness was only possible from within the rules. Chris surprised us by not taking a slap shot; instead he made a beautiful assist. All of his talents, however, were used within the rules.

An outsider might find the rules of hockey confining, restricting the freedom of the players, even keeping their talent on a leash. What if Chris had picked up the puck and hurled it into the net? That would have been a surprise. But only the kind of surprise that is a disappointment. No one would have celebrated the puck going into the net. No matter how accurate the throwing arm of Chris, throwing the puck would never be seen as greatness. Because it is outside the rules of hockey, it would be seen as dangerous, making a penalty the only reasonable outcome. Greatness comes from within the rules, not in spite of the rules.

It is only the outsider that finds the rules of hockey confining. Those who play hockey, or are fans of hockey, know that the rules only give boundaries of behavior, of play, and are not confining at all. The players and fans accept and submit to the rules. The outrageous thrill is to see greatness present itself from within the *confines* of the rules. Perhaps one could say that hockey is bigger on the ice than off.

It is just this way with the Church. The rules add boundaries, but are not confining. Greatness comes from those who incorporate the rules into the everyday goings on of life. Breaking the rules does not prove greatness; it only draws the penalty of sin. It was G.K. Chesterton who said:

> Catholic doctrine and discipline may be walls; but they are the walls of a playground....We might fancy some children playing on the flat grassy top of some tall island in the sea. So long as there was a wall round the cliff's edge they could fling themselves into every frantic game and make the place the noisiest of nurseries. But the walls were knocked down, leaving the naked peril of the precipice. They did not fall over; but when their friends returned to them they were all huddled in terror in the centre of the island; and their song had ceased.[7]

---

[7] G.K. Chesterton, Orthodoxy "Authority and the Adventurer" (New York: Dover Publications Inc., 2004) 138.

The boundaries, the rules, bring freedom.

So, to recall the slap shot—it still seems like an understatement to call it a great play. It was profound, stunning, shocking, breathtaking, overwhelming—a joy to see. It was, for certain, the most exquisite play I have ever seen.

And to recall the most exquisite lives—we only need to look to the Saints. They didn't achieve greatness by cheating, lying, stealing, sinning. They achieved it by overcoming sin, by incorporating the rules, the teachings, into their lives. What makes their lives profound, stunning, shocking, breathtaking, overwhelming, and a joy to witness is that they achieved greatness from within the rules, not in spite of the rules. For certain, they lived the most exquisite lives.

Ah—but isn't living the life of a saint really too much to ask of our children? Aren't the confines of the Commandments too heavy for our children? I suppose you could ask if the slap shot of a man should ever be entrusted to a boy? Chris gave up his rest periods only to learn the rules of hockey more deeply. He accepted a certain pressure from the Gopher players as the teaching intensified. As a result, he flourished.

There is a wonderful paradox in teaching your children to submit to the teachings of the Church. They will experience a wild freedom, and they will flourish *because* of the Commandments, not *in spite* of them.

Chapter Sixteen

HOCKEY IS FUN

A hockey mom once pointed out a "universal truth" of hockey when she said, "But Alyssa, the difference between hockey and the Mass is…hockey is fun." Ah, how beautiful! She was so good to point this out to me. And she was right, wasn't she?

"Yes, you are so right, hockey is fun…but not if you don't know what's going on. Then it's just a hard bench in a cold place and you find yourself looking at your watch, wondering how much longer this can go on."

Think about Grandma, who doesn't know the first thing about hockey. She is there in obligation to her grandchild. To her, hockey is a cold hard metal bench in a cold place. It's the same thing over and over, all the time. There are a lot of skaters doing a lot of running around for seemingly nothing. There are a couple of guys in odd outfits making funny movements with their arms, and the arm positions are supposed to mean something. In order to watch Suzy, Grandma has been told to watch #8. Just when she thinks she has an eye on #8, she can no longer find #8. No one told her about line changes. Okay, Grandma, just follow the puck. "I can't see the puck—it goes too fast and it's too small. Why don't they make it bigger and a brighter color?"

And what about all this sitting and standing? All of a sudden everyone is standing and cheering. When Grandma finally stands up and is able to get someone's attention to ask what just happened, everyone sits down again. She understood to stand during the opening hymn; everyone stands at the anthem, that's the easy part. Then there are assorted other responses to the plays. Some plays elicit groans, others gasps; how is Grandma to know which one to do when? If there is a script, everyone seems to know it but her. There is a collective breath-holding, then an exclamation, "Way to block it." But Grandma can't see the puck; she has no idea if a shot on goal was blocked or not.

Grandma is a bit overcome when she gasps, "Is that child bleeding? Isn't this game a little violent?"

A parent seated behind taps her on the shoulder, leans in, and seems a little too nonchalant when he says, "It isn't hockey until someone bleeds."

Horrified, Grandma is looking at her watch wondering how long until she has fulfilled her obligation. She wishes she were warming a bench, but the hard metal only seems colder as she sits, there is no back support, and, by the way, that liquid cardboard her son tried to pass off to her was *not* hot chocolate. The buzzer goes off and after a start, she feels an overwhelming relief. "It's over."

Her son seems to apologize when he says, "That was just the end of the first period."

Hockey means nothing to Grandma if she has never been catechized. Instead, it is just an obligation she must fulfill "for the kids." It seems that she is stuck in some odd time warp where the clock never moves.

✝

Perhaps G.K. Chesterton was speaking directly to Grandma when he said that it's all meaningless...unless you know what it means.[8] Hockey is fun...just not if you haven't been catechized in it.

The Mass becomes the same cold hard bench in a cold place, or a blazing hot place or an overly air-conditioned place if you are

---

[8] G.K. Chesterton. *Collected Works of G.K. Chesterton*, Volume 21 "The Resurrection of Rome" (San Francisco: Ignatius Press, 1990) 451.

uncatechized. It makes sense to stand at the opening hymn, but why all the sitting and standing and kneeling? And what's with the guy in the odd outfit moving his arms around? It doesn't look like it means anything. If you are uncatechized in the Faith, the Mass is the same thing over and over, all the time. It becomes a place where you continually look at your watch and wonder if it will ever end. You are only there to fulfill an obligation "for the kids."

Unfortunately, you feel trapped outside of time.

✝

So what if we are just like Grandma and don't know the first thing about hockey? Be not afraid, hockey has already thought of this!

I have a friend—let's call her Melissa Halsne, since that's her name. Poor Melissa did not come from a hockey family. Please join me in a moment of silence.

Melissa happened to marry into hockey. Sure it was a conflict, but love can conquer all. If her husband Mike, a former high school skater, wanted to join a town team or play some sort of intramural hockey, it was no problem with Melissa. At the time of their marriage vows, the chance of having little skaters seemed so far off as not to be important. But the years always go a bit faster than we imagine and Melissa found herself with a young skater on her hands.

To say that her younger son Jake took to the ice would be an understatement. Soon Melissa found herself at ice arenas all over the metro. What she saw was a clump of skaters, chasing a nearly invisible puck, while the whole time Melissa was having to sit on a hard bench in a cold place. Her husband and boys lived, breathed, slept, dreamed, and played hockey. Because she didn't understand, however, she felt unable to join all the hockey excitement that surrounded her. She couldn't go on living this way!

Be not afraid; hockey was ready for Melissa. Adult catechesis was the answer.

Melissa joined the moms' hockey league. She was not seeking

some fame for which she had always longed. She did not join because she was finally fulfilling a lifelong dream of dragging her middle-aged, bad kneed, arthritic body out onto a frozen surface—especially seeing as how she had never strapped on a pair of skates previously. She did it, not for herself and her own dreams, but for her children—her family. And in the end, it was a benefit to her as well.

As a result of the adult catechesis, at last Melissa could understand hockey. She understood her son's position on the ice. She could finally see the puck because she came to anticipate its movement. She understood the responses, the cheering and gasping. She could join as her husband and sons were speaking about hockey at dinner. When they watched the Minnesota Gopher and Wild games on television, she enjoyed them with her family.

Melissa wasn't satisfied with her hockey ignorance. It didn't serve her or her family to remain ignorant. Instead, she dragged her middle-aged, bad kneed, arthritic body out onto the hard cold ice. She strapped on the skates for the first time and she dug into the teachings of hockey. Soon she was able to understand and participate in hockey. Melissa got into the game; she put on hockey. This served her and her family, and she even found herself explaining the game to others who didn't understand it.

There are two great truths of hockey that Melissa learned: adult catechesis leads to family catechesis and family harmony. And she learned the other great truth of hockey: it's not hockey until someone bleeds.

✝

If the Mass is thought to be just a personal obligation, chances are that adult catechesis is in order.

If you are just fulfilling the obligation "for the kids," the chances are that they will do the same, just fulfill an obligation for their kids when it's time, and their kids will do the same. Generations of

Catholics will be baptized and taken to Mass with no real idea of what is taking place. The sacraments will become just a rote exercise.

Generations will be looking at their watches wondering when it will be over. What a shame. What a shame that we look at our watches, what a shame that our children will do the same, and what a shame for the future generations who will look at their watches as well. But the Mass is not about time. It is about Eternity.

When we take our children to be baptized, our hope for them is that they have a better grasp of the Faith than we have ourselves. At their baptism, we would never pray that they would grow to be bored with the Faith, that they would never know what the Mass means, and that they would only go through the motions for their own children. There is nowhere in the Baptismal Rite where we pray that our children see the Mass as a hard bench in a cold place and that they would focus on their watches the whole time that they are "there for the kids."

At their baptisms, our hope for our children is at a particularly beautiful height. We pray for them to live their lives in communion with the Church. We ask the angels and saints to assist them. We ask the godparents and community to assist in raising the children in the Faith. Yet, in our own lives we allow the Mass to remain a hard bench in a cold place. We allow the sacraments to be rote. We allow boredom to rule our Faith.

Grandma attends games every now and then. But imagine if she knew what was taking place in front of her! She would come to understand that because hockey is always the "same," it is never the same. Imagine the thrill for her if she were able to really *see* Suzy skate. And if she were not able to make it to the game, imagine the phone conversations between Grandma and Suzy after the game. Imagine Suzy telling her own children about hockey and about the special bond it fostered between her and her grandma.

As parents, we see the merits of adult catechesis in hockey. We see the merits in the moms' hockey league, but we understand further that if there is no moms' hockey league available, we still are responsible to catechize ourselves. There are basic hockey books at the library to check out; we can look up hockey rules on the computer; we can "join" a hockey study group by chatting with other parents before and during the game. We seek to live, breath, sleep, dream, and even at times, play hockey.

We never want future generations to go to hockey only out of obligation. We hope for so much more for them. Yet, when it comes to the Catholic Church, we are somehow satisfied with our boredom. We give no thought to whether our boredom is affecting our children. We give no thought, as we look at our watches for the twentieth time in Mass, that our grandchildren and great-grandchildren will follow our example.

There is Catholic adult catechesis available to us, but will we seek it? Our parishes may have specific programs, but even if they don't, there are tremendous resources available, beginning with the big green book, otherwise known as *The Catechism of the Catholic Church*. Crack it open, discover your Faith and the Faith of your children. It is time to put on the Faith.

The Mass does take place outside of time, yet paradoxically, in time. Not in the heavy obligation sort of way, but in the heavenly oblation sort of way. You will look at your watch—but only at the end, when you wonder where the time went. Once you have been catechized, the mystery of the Mass opens and becomes, in another paradox, a deeper mystery. Because the Mass is always the "same," it is never the same. You are no longer just warming a bench; you are participating in the Perfect Prayer. And you understand that the Mass isn't the Mass until Someone bleeds!

Chapter Seventeen

HERB BROOKS

It was February 22, 1980, a Friday night, and like many Friday nights at the time, I had a babysitting job. Before my ride arrived, we were watching the early news. They told us to look away if we didn't want to see it, but I just couldn't and had to look—the USA Men's Olympic Hockey Team had won against the Soviets! The game was to be broadcast an hour or so later. The father of the children I was to babysit arrived; they were going to a party that evening to watch the game.

Being an over-excited and highly demonstrative 14-year-old, I didn't exactly have a poker face. When the father spoke of the upcoming game, I excitedly said, "I know who won!" He emphatically begged, "Don't tell me!" So I didn't say a word for at least two and a half seconds, but then I couldn't help but burst out, "We won!" He was crestfallen but still kind.

Once we arrived at the house, he ushered his wife out the door quickly so I wouldn't ruin her evening as well. It wasn't long until the game began, and I had a big TV all to myself, or so I thought. His daughters were aged five and three. They were utterly uninterested in the game and kept begging me to change it. Of course, I refused. We had a tea party and played dollies while I watched the game. They were shocked each time I jumped up to cheer.

Near the end of the game, they would cheer with me just to join in. And then we heard, "Do you believe in miracles? Yes!" It was a glorious moment.

When the parents came home, the father immediately told me, "You didn't ruin it for me. The game was incredible. Were you able to watch it with the girls?" I nodded and he said, "Good." It was incredible; a memory I'll never forget. The team became family to all of us, and at the helm was Herb Brooks. We all loved Herb Brooks.

✝

It was August 11, 2003, a Monday afternoon, and like all other Monday afternoons, I was at work. We heard that Herb Brooks was in a car accident and had died. It was an odd feeling knowing that this great man died in relative anonymity on the side of the road. Other traffic would be routed around him; they would have seen the wreckage, but not have known who was in the car. How could the great Herb Brooks come to such an end? We wanted so much more, so much better, for our hero.

We began reminiscing about where we had been for the Olympic game against the Soviets, the Miracle on Ice. There were some younger people who didn't know Herb Brooks; we did our best to tell them and to convey the magnitude of the loss. Herb's loss wasn't just for Minnesota, and not even just a loss for hockey. Instead, this was a loss for the world, and in a particular way for Americans. He had given us one of our greatest victories and by doing so, he became a beloved figure in our homes and in our hearts. How grateful I am for the gifts Herb Brooks gave to hockey, to America, and to me on that Friday night when I was fourteen.

✝

Minnesota is the State of Hockey and one of the greats, one of the greatest greats, was a native son. Hockey is better for there having been a Herb Brooks. The man has become a model for coaches and players alike. As I mentioned earlier, there is a beautifully horrific hockey drill named after him, Herbies. But there is so much more. Awards and streets have been named for him. There is at least one statue of him. The Olympic ice arena in Lake Placid is now named Herb Brooks Arena. St. Cloud State University is now the home of the Herb Brooks National Hockey Center. There has been a movie made about him and his 1980 team. And he lives on in the hearts of all of us, especially as we speak about his greatness.

Herb Brooks was like the rest of us; he was given one life. What he did was to see the opportunities, especially the opportunities in hockey, and to seize them, not just for himself, but for others as well. Perhaps his most notable call was to that 1980 Olympic team as they were about to go onto the ice to meet the Soviets.

The coach pulled out a yellow scrap of paper and said, "You were born to be a player. You were meant to be here. This moment is yours."[9]

Coach Brooks gave his team the age-old advice, "Be not afraid!" His team left the safety of the locker room. They went to the ice where they would give everything for hockey and America; they went out for the sacrifice of the game. And after one of the great battles, they were victorious over the Soviets.

Like the saints, Herb Brooks called others to greatness. At the time of the game, he wasn't imagining greatness for himself; instead he saw greatness in the team. But it didn't end there. Herb Brooks was the coach for the USA hockey team; he was calling his team to be great Americans, and by doing so, he was also calling all Americans to a new greatness. None of it would have been possible if he hadn't called his team to do the everyday, ordinary work of playing hockey first.

Brooks and his team set out to play an ordinary hockey game, under ordinary hockey rules, in an ordinary hockey rink, with

---

[9] Wayne Coffey, *The Boys of Winter: The Untold Story of a Coach, a Dream, and the 1980 U.S. Olympic Hockey Team* (New York: Crown Publishers, 2005) 25.

ordinary goal nets, lines, and ice. They knew that the circumstances surrounding the game were extraordinary, but to get caught up in circumstances would be to lose. The hard work of an ordinary game must be undertaken.

The players must be focused on the job at hand and not future fame or endorsement deals. If the players had calculated merely the vision of future greatness, by focusing on things like the honor of lighting the Olympic Cauldron in 2002, they never would have won. A part of Brooks' greatness was his ability to focus on the immediate picture, the opportunity at hand, the work that was in front of him and his team, and that work was to win a hockey game. And greatness came because Brooks and his team did what they had been called to do, play hockey. They did not possess super powers in order to accomplish the task; they used only their natural talents, honed over years of drilling and games and exhaustion. They had honed those talents to the highest degree possible. It was only by doing their best in the ordinary things that ultimate greatness was achieved.

The late Herb Brooks had lived a life of heroic hockey virtue. He embodied hockey. He knew the rules of hockey; as a coach he imparted all of hockey and its rules to his skaters. He understood that the "confines" of hockey allowed for a great freedom. In the constellation of hockey's heroes, Herb Brooks is one of the brightest stars.

$$+$$

It was April 2, 2005, a cool spring day, a day like many other spring days, except for one thing. I was sitting outside writing in my journal, recording my observations of what was happening in front of me. I was in St. Peter's Square in Rome and the Holy Father, Pope John Paul II, was in his apartment dying. Throughout the day the crowds had increased, and there were thousands of us there at 9:37 p.m., when at last he went Home. It was a most incredible day, one of sorrow and joy. My journal entry began before 9 a.m. that morning and ended sometime after midnight, after the prayer vigil. The one line from the journal that comes to mind is this:

One life—that is all this man had—one life—same as all of us.

The man who became Pope John Paul II didn't set out in his youth to have thousands of people standing outside his window when he died—that was just the outcome of his life of faith. He was a man who saw the everyday ordinary opportunities in front of him. He answered the call to become a parish priest and to do the everyday work of a priest. He answered the call to become a bishop and cardinal, and later to become the Holy Father.

When he was elected, he came to the balcony and told the world, "Be not afraid!"

John Paul II acted on what was presented to him. He wasn't given super powers with which to move through life. Instead he was given one life, same as all of us, and he used his in the highest manner possible. By living within the "confines" of the Commandments, he was free—free to live a life of heroic virtue. Teenagers flocked to him especially during World Youth Days, where he imparted a radical message. He told them, "Be not afraid!" and called them to live in the highest manner possible. He called them to do the ordinary greatly; by doing so, they were to live lives of heroic virtue.

+

Herb Brooks is a giant among hockey heroes. We will gladly teach our children about Herb Brooks and his, and one of America's, greatness victories. By holding him up to our children, we give them a model to look to in hockey. What do our children have in common with Herb Brooks? One life. He was given one life, same as all of us.

Pope Blessed John Paul II is among the Communion of Saints; he is rightly placed there. Will we gladly teach our children about JPII and his greatness, and his great victory, his eternal triumph in heaven?

Perhaps we will say that our children have nothing in common with JPII. Ah, they have one thing in common for certain. We all do. One life. He was given one life. When teaching children as they prepare for First Holy Communion, I show them the picture of JPII on his Communion day. He was the same young child, preparing to receive Christ in the Sacrament.

There are so many things our children have in common with the Communion of Saints. There are patron Saints for everything. If you are looking for a model for your child from the world of athletics, how about St. Paul? He encouraged us to "fight the good fight." John Paul II was an athlete. The lives of the Saints are fascinating. By giving the Saints to our children, we give them models to emulate. To find common ground between a Saint and your child, begin with the truth that everyone has one life.

In essence, Herb Brooks also told his team, "Be not afraid!" They responded with a victory in an ordinary game of hockey that happened to have extraordinary ramifications. He called his team to greatness and they responded with an emphatic, "Yes!"

John Paul II told his flock, "Be not afraid!" Teenagers flocked to see an octogenarian; he called them to greatness and they responded with an emphatic, "Yes!"

You must now call your children to greatness—not just in big things, but also in the small and mundane. We must expect them to do the small things greatly in order that they can one day respond properly to, and be ready for, the big things.

They are to live lives of heroic virtue, and they are capable of responding with an emphatic, "Yes!" But they must be called, and called continuously. They need Saints to turn to for models; we, as their parents, must become models of heroic virtue. Their one life is not to be wasted. Instead, it is to be lived at the highest level possible—especially in the day-in, day-out, everyday ordinary goings on, for this is where the saints are made.

Chapter Eighteen

THE TICKET

All the great disciples of hockey teach their skaters about heroes of hockey, with particular attention to Herb Brooks. It could even be said that the disciples *drill* the teaching of Herb Brooks into their skaters as they mandate more *Herbies*. But from time to time, there will be a skater who does not know about Herb Brooks. Luckily, her grandpa knows about him and the 1980 team; soon the young skater, his granddaughter, will know as well.

"Sit down, child. Grandpa is going to teach you a little something about hockey."

The young skater appeals to her mother, eyes pleading, and voice with a touch of whining, "Do I have to?"

A knowing look shared with grandpa, then to the child, "Listen to Grandpa, this is important."

Grandpa first sets the stage. "The time was 1980. We were at the height of the Cold War." He explains the political atmosphere as the child waits impatiently, wondering what politics could ever have to do with hockey. Grandpa goes on to explain that the Olympics were on American soil, or rather ice. There were the so-called amateurs from the Soviet Union who were considered unbeatable and better than any NHL team. It was a foregone conclusion that they would take home the gold medal; the only apparent competition was for the silver. Coach Herb Brooks had what *seemed* like a rag-tag group of college boys from around the US who had never before skated together.

The young skater hasn't exactly been gripped by grandpa's story, but she knows enough to pay attention when her mother says it's important. Grandpa says that this is a story of David and Goliath. She doesn't exactly know what that means, but she continues to listen.

As the USA Men's hockey team took the ice at the opening of the Olympics, there were very few fans in the seats. But an odd thing happened; the boys kept winning. In fact, the boys weren't skating like boys; they were skating like men, and it seemed as though they had been playing together *since* they were boys. The stands began to fill with fans—more at each succeeding game. As the excitement grew, there was a new cheer: USA—USA—*USA!*

Soon, their games became the hottest ticket, and millions watched the broadcasts. *Everyone* became a hockey fan, and every conversation was about Herb Brooks and *our* USA hockey team. Then the craziest thing happened: *we* advanced to the medal round. But we had to beat the Soviets, who had shut down the US team in a pre-Olympic exhibition game 10-3. Was it a foregone conclusion that the US would lose again? There was a crazy glimmer of hope among Americans—could we do it?

The young skater cannot hide her interest. "Did we win, Grandpa?"

"I'm getting to that."

There was that last-second goal in the first period to tie the game at 2-2. But little to cheer about in the second period as the Soviets dominated. At the buzzer, due to exceptional goaltending by the Americans, the Soviets were only up by one goal. During the third period the Soviets kept their stars on the ice, but Herb had been rotating four lines throughout the game. The US men had fresher legs.

"But did we win?"

"We're almost to that part."

At the start of the third period USA was behind 3-2, but a goal on a power play brought us even; now it was 3-3.

More emphatically, "But did we win?"

"You know, there can be ties in hockey, even Olympic hockey. Let's see what happens."

There was a mistake made by the Soviets, and the USA team seized the opportunity. A 25-foot shot got in, the crowd erupted, and the score was 4-3 USA. What happened next is often referred to as the "tensest 10 minutes in sports." The Soviets could still win in a blowout, they were that good.

Nine minutes and 49 seconds had passed, and then we heard broadcaster Al Michaels say: "Eleven seconds. You got ten seconds, the countdown going on right now.... Five seconds left in the game! *Do you believe in miracles? Yes!*"

"We won! We won! Grandpa, we won!"

"Yes, child, now let me get the newspapers and magazines. You need to meet Herb Brooks and the team. There is even more to the story; we may have beat the Soviets, but we still had to win the gold." After looking at the scrapbook of newspaper articles and magazine covers, grandpa says, "Have your mother pop some corn, there's a movie you need to see."

✝

Grandpa did not just show the movie and forget about it. There was the day when his granddaughter joined him as they went on a pilgrimage. Grandpa took her to Lake Placid, to the arena now named for Herb Brooks.

Now in the arena, he asks her to stand still and *smell* the ice. He tells her to take this all in; you may never be here again. He takes her high into the stands and asks her to picture the crowd. He takes out his wallet and pulls out the ticket stub.

Her eyes widen and she gasps, "Were you here?"

"Yes."

"Where were you sitting?"

"Look at the ticket and find the seat."

After a few minutes looking around for the section number, the row, and the seat, she exclaims, "This was your seat! I'm sitting in your seat!"

"Yes, I was here and now you are here. This is the place of our greatest victory. Take it in with all your senses. One day, you will have the ticket and you will bring your children here."

He continues, "Now listen. Can you hear the crowd? USA—USA—*USA!*"

"Yes."

"Do you believe in miracles?"

They whisper together, "Yes!"

✝

The story of Herb Brooks and our 1980 Olympic Hockey Team is one of the great stories in hockey. Parents teach it, grandparents teach it, and someday children will teach it to their children. It is a timeless story. There is *something* about the underdog. There is *something* about David and Goliath. And there is *something* about a leader calling a team to greatness.

The Church is full of these stories. Perhaps grandma or grandpa has a devotion to Padre Pio. Your parish is named after St. Augustine. The city you live in is named after St. Paul. Your neighbor has a statue of Mary in the garden. The cemetery your children pass on the way to school is named for St. Lawrence. There is a sticker of St. Christopher in the car. And mom uses a holy card of Mother Teresa as a bookmark in her Bible.

When it comes to hockey, intergenerational teaching is welcomed. Parents, grandparents, aunts, uncles, and neighbors are happy to teach and we expect our children to listen.

Yet, when it comes to the Faith, we are often hesitant or unwilling to tell of our devotions. Somehow, we think that anything we relate will just be seen as "crazy talk." When it comes to the Faith, we often disregard grandpa's devotion to Padre Pio. Having St. Paul as a name of our city becomes only a sound. The neighbor's garden with Mary is just a curiosity. And who cares what the cemetery is named, those people are dead anyway. But what if one day we told the story about our devotion to St. Bernadette, telling it calmly, without apology, without embarrassment, instead, breathing *life* into the story.

We spend little or no time *giving* our children the Communion of Saints. Herb Brooks has an exercise named for him, *Herbies*. Our children *know* this exercise. But do they know the Ignatian Exercises? Have they heard of Dominican Spirituality, Franciscan Charity, or Benedictine Hospitality? How about Thomistic Thought? Or even the simplest Marian Devotions?

We might take our children to Lake Placid, or the Hockey Hall of Fame in Canada, or the US Hockey Hall of Fame, or the Minnesota Hockey Hall of Fame. Our child's travel team might be going to Hibbing, and as they enter the rink, we remind them that this is where all the Micheletti brothers played. Or we may be in the Roseau rink where the David and Goliath story is alive and well, as Roseau consistently beats teams from substantially larger schools. There may be a college or professional skater who came from their local rink, and when our children are struggling on the ice, we remind them of this.

We take hockey pilgrimages, but what of spiritual pilgrimages? Have we taken our children to a Marian shrine? Have we taken them to a side altar to St. Joseph? Whose relics are in the altar at our parish, and what do we know of that Saint? Why do we call Therese the Little Flower, and why do we call Aquinas the Doctor of the Eucharist? Do we have any idea where our parish priest celebrated his first Mass of Thanksgiving and have we ever visited that parish to give thanks for his vocation?

Chances are that your own parish would be a great place to take a spiritual pilgrimage. Ask your pastor, or a staff member, or a lifetime parishioner to take you around. Study the art in the stained glass windows. See if you can learn why St. Paul is nearly always shown with a sword, St. Peter with keys, and St. Joseph with a lily. Why do so many baptismal fonts have eight sides? How come there are always holy water fonts at the doors?

Have we *taken in* the Church with all our senses? Have we asked our children to do the same?

Grandpa first taught his granddaughter about Herb Brooks in a story. Then he took her on a pilgrimage. His granddaughter will never forget the story, which became an indelible memory when she smelled the ice, sat in the seat, and held the ticket.

The Communion of Saints is full of heroes for our children, and pilgrimages are as close as your own parish. The greatest story ever told is still being told through your children—and we are all hoping for the same ending…"Do you believe in miracles? Yes!"

Chapter Nineteen

THE JERSEY

On January 9, 1979, the #4 hockey jersey of Bobby Orr was retired at Boston Garden, his number never to be worn again by a Bruins player. The crowd would not stop applauding. Bobby Orr could not give his thank-you speech until he donned his jersey one more time. Even after his talk the applause was sustained, and much of the rest of the evening's program had to be scrapped; the crowd just couldn't stop applauding for Bobby Orr, one of hockey's greats.

My young friend Jake has a book signed by Bobby Orr. Signed photos and cards and game jerseys and old hockey sticks and ticket stubs and such are referred to as sports memorabilia. Every sport has memorabilia, and there is a large market for it, but what is the *real* worth of these things?

Something about sports memorabilia captivates us. Why are autographs of our sports heroes so valuable? Why should we care if we have an *actual* game jersey of a professional skater or just a reproduction? Of course, this goes well beyond sports into celebrity of all sorts, even into our nation's past. For example, a signature of Abraham Lincoln is said to be worth about $25,000. But *why?* Wouldn't a photocopy of his signature be just as good? Simply, no. The answer to the *"why"* is rather simple: the original signature is a *part* of Abraham Lincoln; the photocopy is not.

Why do we care to have a part of Abraham Lincoln? It's because of who he is and was, and the life he led. If we are able to touch or trace our finger along his signature, or just to *see* the signature in person, we feel we have somehow *met* Abraham Lincoln. Even if we can't *verbalize* why, we instinctively know the value of his signature; its worth is far beyond money.

There is something in all of this zeal for memorabilia about the *closeness* to the actual person. For example, a ticket stub to a winning game is one thing, but having caught the ball from the game-winning home run is quite another. Then, if it were possible, to get the ball signed by the player who hit it out of the park, better still. But a photo with you, the player, and the now signed ball would be a priceless keepsake. The closeness to the player is key. Something the players touched, used, wore, signed, etc.—these things are worth more. Ask any Elvis fan what a trip to Graceland means. A friend of mine speaks of the three times she saw Elvis in concert and the many times she has been to Graceland on the anniversary of his death. (Oddly enough, I speak of *having* a friend who saw Elvis three times in concert and who has gone to Graceland a number of times on the anniversary of his death. Perhaps one day my niece will speak of her aunt who had a friend who saw Elvis three times in concert and often went to Graceland on the anniversary of his death.)

What does all this mean? Sports and celebrity memorabilia are types of relics.

Knowing someone who knows someone who has been at an Elvis concert is better than just knowing that people went to his concerts. Having been at an Elvis concert is better than hearing him on the radio. *Being* at Graceland is better than looking at pictures of it. *Being* in Lake Placid at the Herb Brooks Arena is better than seeing it in a movie. And then, being able to *touch* something that they touched, to *see* something of theirs, or to stand at the grave of one of our heroes is somehow to *meet* them.

+

When I was a young, I was looking at my baby book and those of my siblings. My mother had done a remarkable job keeping eight baby books up to date. There was something extraordinary in seeing the locks of hair from each of my siblings. I was the youngest and never knew my siblings when they had that wispy, soft baby hair. Each lock was in a little thin plastic bag. One by one, I would run my finger over the thin plastic, *feeling* the hair of my siblings, and somehow *meeting* them as babies.

I had noticed it before, but this time my mother was with me as I looked at my own baby book. So I asked her, "Where is my lock of hair?" She responded, "It should be right there." She came and helped me look through the book. My mother realized that she had never kept a lock of my hair. She told me that she had always left my hair long, and when it finally was cut she must have just forgotten. We both had that silent moment, the sort of moment where you just sit with something for a minute. We were both a little sorry, but neither was upset. My mother then said, "We could cut a lock of your hair now." And then almost in unison we both said, "No, it's not the same."

There is *something* about a baby's lock of hair. There is *something* about the old tradition of a lock of hair in a locket around the neck of a loved one. These are the sorts of family relics that we all have, and there is *something* about them, and that something is quite wonderful. And yet, why do we think it is strange that Catholics care about the relics of Saints?

+

There was a time when my students and I were at a lecture with the great Dominican, Fr. Paul Murray. The students were able to ask him questions, and one student asked him who his favorite Saint is.

He began to tell them of St. Catherine of Siena. At times he spoke of her in tender terms, at other times with humor, at other times with a sort of awe. I knew what was happening, but it was fantastic to hear the students tell me of it later. "Father spoke of St. Catherine as if they were *friends*."

"Yes, exactly, they are friends. They are great friends."

✝

Whenever in Rome or Siena I like to pray with the relics of St. Catherine of Siena. Her body is under the main altar at Santa Maria Sopra Minerva. Because she was beloved by all of Rome *and* all of Siena, however, her body is in Rome and her head in Siena. In either place, by being and praying with her relics, I am meeting a member of the Communion of Saints.

My friendship began with Catherine of Siena in 2002 while on a tour of Italy. We first met in Siena and later again in Rome. She has been a powerful intercessor for me on a number of occasions.

✝

Bobby Orr's jersey is of the utmost importance to hockey. It does not hang in Boston Garden as a simple jersey, a piece of fabric. Instead, his retired jersey is a reminder of *Bobby Orr* and his career. It is a reminder of the glorious days when Orr was on the ice. It is a reminder to every child of a dream. Bobby Orr lived a life of heroic dedication to hockey. His was a life of talent honed by amazing discipline and drive. Orr did not just stumble across hockey greatness, he *worked* for hockey greatness.

Rightly, the retiring of a jersey has become a sort of canonization. The day the jersey is to be retired becomes a sort of holy day. To arrive at this day of canonization, a player's career must be scrutinized and found to be lacking nothing. The actual day of the canonization is full of ceremony and pageantry. It's a day to remember, and the retired jersey hung in the arena becomes a sort of beacon to all of hockey.

But hockey relics don't rest merely in old arenas. Think of the newer arena down the street. When it opened, a hometown skater who made it to the pros gave a game jersey to be hung in the lobby. Although the building is new, already present is the history of those great hockey players who have come before; already, this new arena is a part of a much older tradition, and this particular relic will inspire new generations of skaters.

We ask our young skaters to look to skaters like Orr. "Do it like Orr did it." "Orr lost at times too, but he *never* gave up. You can do it!" There may even be times when parents *ad lib* a bit when they say, "I bet Bobby Orr never complained about eating his broccoli." We ask our children to look to the greats, to emulate them, to *be* like them. There is this sort of connection not just from our memory of the greats, but also from their relics. And if skaters know the lifetime statistics of Bobby Orr and perhaps some trivia about him, they have somehow become *friends* with Bobby Orr.

+

There is something so very natural about our desire for relics. What an honor it would be to have Abraham Lincoln's signature, or to have Bobby Orr's jersey, or signature. Wouldn't it great to touch a pair of Herb Brooks' skates? But fame is not a prerequisite for keeping relics. We all keep family relics. We hold onto grandma's teacups, grandpa's pipe, and those simple locks of hair from our children. We entrust these relics to the next generation. Somehow our children and grandchildren come to *know* their ancestors in the passing down of the relics. The relics are somehow the keepers of the stories of the lives of those who have gone before us. And we speak of the day that we will meet again in heaven.

Once a friend told me that she just couldn't relate to the Communion of the Saints. The only one she believed in was Blessed Teresa of Calcutta because she had lived during our lifetime. I asked if she would teach her children about Teresa. Yes, she would. And would she teach her grandchildren? Yes, she would. Would she hope that they passed the stories to their children? Yes, she would.

But how were they to believe in Teresa if she had not lived in their lifetime? Because of the passing of the stories. And what if you could have a letter signed by Mother Teresa? Or a rosary that she used? Or a lock of her hair? It is not just the passing of the stories, but also the passing of the relics.

We naturally do this in our families, and the Church does this for Her family as well, the mystical body. It begins with individuals whose lives have been recognized for heroic virtue. Later, there is a beatification, followed one day by a canonization; these are days filled with ceremony and pageantry. We come to Mass to celebrate Holy Days and Feast Days in remembrance of the Saints. We pray with their relics, and ask for their intercession with Christ. And then we pass these stories to the multitude of generations to come.

Could Father Murray really be a friend with St. Catherine of Siena? Yes.

Could coming into contact with the relics of St. Catherine really be of worth? Yes.

Why?

We believe in the Communion of Saints and the Resurrection of the Body, and there is this incredible knowledge that one day, God willing, we will meet Saints like Catherine of Siena again in heaven, where we will continue our friendship. In hockey, we look to a scrapbook of Herb Brooks, or the opportunity to touch his skates, perhaps hoping one day, God willing, to meet him. At the end of time, we will be reunited with our bodies; the body of Catherine that we have prayed next to on earth will be the body, now Glorified, that we meet in heaven. Meanwhile, on earth we can visit her relics, pray with her, and look forward with great joy to that day in heaven.

Chapter Twenty

TEAMWEAR

There is a 14-letter word that makes every Catholic nervous, which is why I am nervous to say it now. I'll understand if after reading it, you close the book and walk away. But before you do that, let me first mention that in hockey we *always* do what this word says. Here goes...*Evangelization.*

Are you still there? Is anyone out there?

Perhaps you think that I have gone too far. You were with me for Herb Brooks, the commissioner and the governing body, Abraham Lincoln (and you sort of liked that I slipped Elvis into the analogy). You even tolerated the penalty box. But this, this evangelization talk, this is going too far. But before you mark me as some kind of crazy zealot, let me say one word in my defense: Teamwear!

Yes, that's right, I said, "Teamwear!"

"Always be ready to give an explanation to anyone who asks you for a reason for your hope." (1 Peter 3:15)[10]

In case you are still a little dazed, let me say it again: "Teamwear!"

The on-ice uniform with the team name on the front and the skater's name on the back is not enough for the typical hockey skater. Hockey is not merely something that skaters do on a sheet of ice surrounded by boards and glass and shut away in refrigerated

---

[10] *The Holy Bible*, New American Bible (NAB) (New York: Catholic Book Publishing Co., 1992). [All other Biblical citations throughout taken from NAB, unless otherwise noted.]

buildings. That's just where the sacrifice of the game takes place. But hockey itself is something that reaches far beyond the confines of a frozen rink. And how does it do this? Simply, by teamwear.

The on-ice uniform is not worn off the ice except for the jersey, which may be worn on special occasions. But skaters rightly love hockey; they live, breathe, sleep, dream, play, and even *wear* hockey. The on-ice uniform is just not enough. Skaters want and need sweatpants with the team name up and down the leg. They need stocking caps, t-shirts, sweatshirts, jackets—both winter and spring—and scarves and mittens. Ah, but this is not all. To get all that equipment to and from the hockey rink, you need giant equipment bags. Sure, you can purchase bags without the team name on them, but why would you? The equipment bags are *huge* and a great place to show your team name, which must be printed as large as it can possibly be.

Is teamwear in itself enough? No. Teamwear is better if enhanced in some fashion. Skaters want their own names embroidered on teamwear, making these items somehow even better. Why teamwear? Simply, it is an *outward sign* of an *inward reality*. Perhaps now you think that I really have gone too far—teamwear is just something fun for the kids; it's not really an evangelization tool, right?

✝

Permit me to use a shocking symbol to illustrate my point. Were you to see someone wearing the swastika, you would be instinctively repulsed. The actual swastika symbol itself is quite simple, but the *meaning* of it is anything but simple. There is a horrific history attached to it.

Were we to see someone wearing a t-shirt with the swastika, we would immediately attach the history of the swastika to the person wearing it. We would *never* think, "I bet he is wearing that because he is really opposed to the ideals that symbol represents; by wearing the t-shirt, he's pointing out how wrong they are." In addition, we would *never* think, "He must not have had anything else clean to wear today." No, we don't have t-shirts like that in the bottom of our drawers, and we would *never* wear one, even if it were the last clean shirt. If we found one, we wouldn't take it to the second-hand store, we wouldn't give it away, and we wouldn't hand it down when we grew out of it. If somehow we were to acquire such a garment, our first urge would be to destroy it immediately.

We instinctively know that a person wearing the swastika assents to all it stands for, and he wants others to know that he assents to those teachings. The shirt is an *outward sign* of an *inward reality*. In a sense, by wearing it, he hopes to evangelize, to attract and convert others to the horrible ideals he holds. Wearing such an item is purposeful.

✝

Hockey teamwear is an *outward sign* of an *inward reality*. Skaters wear teamwear from their own teams or teams they support. Should we see skaters or fans wearing teamwear from another team, we can suspect they lost a bet. For example, if the Huskies win over the Gophers, then I will wear a Husky jersey. (Perish the thought.) And if the Gophers win over the Huskies, you will wear a Gopher jersey. In fact, we *love* these bets. Why? Because of the humorous contradiction created. You now have to wear my team's jersey. It is humorous precisely because it is *not* an outward sign of an inward reality. The embarrassment comes if someone who knows you sees you in this contradiction. Or, perhaps worse yet, someone who doesn't know you sees you; somehow you are evangelizing to them that your team is the Gophers. You instinctively want to tell everyone that you are really a Huskies fan. Ah, but there is great joy for me in knowing that you are evangelizing for my team when you don't really mean to. This sort of turnabout is not just fair play—it's a riot!

Teamwear *means* something. You would never wear the opposition's teamwear to a game; you wouldn't even own any. In addition, teamwear is worn all the time. No one complains about wearing teamwear. No one complains that everyone else will be wearing the same thing. No one scoffs at a fan who is always in teamwear, game after game in teamwear. If there is a weekend tournament, it is expected that teamwear will be worn through the weekend—so what if there is a mustard stain on that, rinse it out at night; get your colors on! There is even a special respect shown to those who persevere in wearing teamwear throughout a losing season. "For better or worse, they are faithful and true fans."

Teamwear is worn everywhere. A skater may wear teamwear alone or in a large group. It is worn to games, to school, to the grocery store, to the park, to church—*everywhere*. More than one coach has warned his team about bad behavior while they are wearing teamwear. They are to be on especially good behavior because they are representing the team. Bad behavior while in teamwear is some-how an endorsement of bad behavior by the team, causing scandal.

And teamwear is worn by practically everyone. Skaters wear it, parents wear it, siblings wear it, grandparents wear it, aunts and uncles wear it—*everyone wears it!* But wait—there's another group wearing teamwear, and they wear it without even giving their consent. That's right—babies wear teamwear! "Oh, the baby looks so cute in the Gopher onesie!" Yes, we dress babies in teamwear before they can even hold up their heads.

And while we are at it, let's talk about picking teams for our children at birth. "In this house we are Gopher fans. No child of mine is going to root for the Huskies." Pity the teens who go against the family and cheer for another team. We spend our time trying to re-catechize them. "Ray, you may think that the Huskies are the right team, but I think if you take a closer look at the complete history and teaching of the Gophers, you will find that your old dad is right, the Gophers are the only team to cheer for." Or perhaps a parent might think, "You're just going through a rebellious stage, trying to find a team that your parents don't cheer for. We haven't lost hope, we know one day you will cheer for the Gophers again." Then in desperation we retrieve the photo album with the pictures of Ray in his Gopher onesie to prove to him that he was once a Gopher fan, in hopes that one day he will return to the fold.

There are families with generations of Gopher fans. Then, one day, the unthinkable happens, a first child goes to college at St. Cloud State and becomes a Huskies fan; there is a murmur in the family. Grandma is clutching her pearls as she whispers, "We've never had a Husky in the family before."

But is teamwear just something we wear? No, we decorate our houses in it! There is more than one house in town that runs the Maroon and Gold Gopher flag up the flagpole. How about the Gopher flannel blanket on the couch, not to mention the one in the back of the car? Speaking of the car, your bumper sticker looks a little worn out; you should really replace it with a new one so it doesn't look so shabby. I can't believe you don't have the Gopher alumni license plate yet. And don't think I didn't notice the matching plastic beer mugs that you brought home from the game. By the way, you owe me five bucks—Hey, cool, I love your Gopher check blanks. Where did you get that signed picture of the 1979 NCAA Gopher championship team? I love how you have it framed, and what a great idea to put it right over the fireplace!

Teamwear is worn and decorates our houses and businesses with pride! Imagine going into the local hamburger joint. A local youth hockey team is there after the game. They all are adorned in teamwear. Imagine an out-of-towner stopping to ask, "What is this hockey you speak of?" Every skater there would be ready to give an explanation. They may be shocked perhaps that there could possibly be a living soul who doesn't know about hockey, but you can easily imagine that the skaters would be ready, and willing, to explain the game that they love so dearly.

"Always be ready to give an explanation to anyone who asks you for a reason for your hope." (1 Peter 3:15)

I once knew two boys, both skaters. Their aunts were from Central America, but came to Minnesota once in the winter. Ice rinks do not feature prominently in Central America. The aunts really had no idea what hockey was. Who evangelized them? The two teenaged boys, and they were thrilled to do it.

✝

As Catholics, we are nervous just at hearing the word, "evangelization." If it is said, it is usually said with a conciliatory voice. "Oh, I hate to bring this up, but it is something we are supposed to talk about. In Confirmation we agreed to do it, and I don't want to really push you, but the bishop does want us to talk about this, but please don't get turned off, just hear me out. I mean, it's not like I'm going to ask you to go and ring your neighbor's doorbell, but we just have to get through this...."

Of course, there is my favorite "excuse" for not evangelizing. "St. Francis told us to preach all the time, and when we have to, use words. See, so I don't really have to *say* anything to evangelize."

What? Are you kidding me? *St. Francis wore teamwear.* We call it his habit. Everyone knew who St. Francis was by his teamwear. His teamwear identified him as Catholic, even if someone saw him from down the street. If he hadn't been wearing teamwear you can bet that he would have used words. And he did use words—his teamwear wasn't an excuse to never use words.

Do you wear Catholic teamwear? Do you wear *outward signs* of an *inward reality?* We are so ready to evangelize in sports, but we cower at the idea of evangelizing in the Faith. We need to wear our faith. It needs to be evident in everything about us. Our faith must be a part of our apparel, that is, it must be *apparent.*

When it is obvious that we are Catholic, that we are not ashamed of it, it will invite reaction. What if someone asks me a question about Catholicism that I don't know? Think about it: what if someone asked you something about hockey that you didn't know? You would admit it, perhaps seek the answer, or point the person to an expert. But you wouldn't be chicken to be *asked.* And you wouldn't be ashamed not to know the answer. It wouldn't make you want to give up on hockey. On the contrary, you would even catechize yourself on that particular hockey question so you would be ready the next time. We profess our loyalty to our teams day in and day out, in private and in public. What's so different about the Catholic Faith?

"Always be ready to give an explanation to anyone who asks you for a reason for your hope." (1 Peter 3:15)

And put on some Catholic teamwear! You never know when you may have the opportunity to evangelize.

Chapter Twenty-One

CAL AND SARAH

One of Sarah Ahlquist's first memories was of the Minnesota High School Hockey Tournament being played on television. She was four-years-old. From that moment, she knew that she loved hockey. A few years later she remembers begging her father to allow her to play hockey.[11]

Cal Ahlquist, her father, grew up as a hockey player. Now he was a father to three daughters and not exactly a fan of girls' hockey. In fact, at the time, girls' hockey didn't exist; girls played "ringette," a game which happened to be played on ice but wasn't hockey. As Cal recalls, Sarah begged for a year or two to play hockey. Sarah recalls begging for four years to play hockey. But Sarah didn't want to be just a skater; she wanted to be a goalie. Cal tried over and over to dissuade her, to no avail. So there was only one thing left to do: rent ice time at the Bloomington Ice Garden.

The Bloomington Ice Garden has a storied history that includes miracles. The 1980 USA Men's Olympic Hockey team had their first practice at the Ice Garden with Herb Brooks…*do you believe in miracles? Yes!* Both Cal and Sarah were hoping for a miracle. Cal was hoping Sarah would abandon her dream to become a goalie;

---

[11] The story of Cal and Sarah, and the quotes in it, are from personal interviews with Cal and Sarah Ahlquist.

Sarah was hoping her father would finally let her be one. There's just no telling what might happen if you begin at the Ice Garden.

Cal gathered all the equipment for a goalie and suited up his daughter. Sarah recalls the moment she finally put on the equipment. "I wasn't nervous at all, just excited." Cal laced up his own skates, and the two of them took the ice. He put Sarah in the net, gave her a few instructions, and said, "If you want to be a goalie, you have to be prepared to take the shots." He skated out a ways, threw down a host of pucks, and proceeded to take shot after shot after shot at Sarah, hoping to cure her of the idea of hockey.

Sarah took every shot—slap shots, angled shots, harder shots, softer shots—every shot her father could give her in the hour. The session was intense, but she began to realize she could do it. "Hey, I'm stopping these shots!" Her dad had rented ice for an hour, and Sarah was in the goal the whole time. At some point the girl in the boy's equipment thought, "This crazy little hair-brained dream might come true." Her excitement grew as the hour progressed.

By the time the hour finished, they had both left everything on the ice. Cal had begun slowly, increased his speed and the velocity of the shots, even making her feel the sting of the slap shot. He went into the crease, banged Sarah around a bit, even bumping her with the stick at times. She needed to have a good feel for being a goalie. He remembers being astonished that she *never* flinched. "She had an uncanny ability to be fearless." When Cal left the ice, his legs hurt, he was out of breath, but he thought he had done it. He'd cured Sarah. He asked, "Now, how do you like hockey?" Her response, "I *love* it!" That hour on the ice had not cured the fever but only intensified it. Now she didn't just *want* to be a goalie, she *had* to be a goalie.

Sarah's catechesis continued with her father, on the flooded and frozen front yard at home. He skated with her for hours, knowing there was something about "raw moves" on a "frozen pond." The catechesis continued on boys' hockey teams; there were no teams for girls. At one tryout, there were eight boys with

Sarah competing for two positions; seven boys were sent home, one boy became the second string goalie, and Sarah was named starting goalie. Soon the idea of girls' high school hockey caught on. As a sophomore in high school, Sarah played on the girls' team. As a junior, she played on the boys' team, and as a senior, she was back with the girls.

By her senior year, the little girl who at the age of four wanted to be "in the net" had become one of the best goalies in Minnesota, with 18 shut-outs during the season. Her team, South St. Paul, had to face the Eagan team in the playoffs to get into the State Tournament. Sarah was in the net against Eagan's Natalie Darwitz, who would become a three-time world champion, a three-time Olympic medalist, and a two-time national champion with the University of Minnesota Golden Gophers. Natalie was unstoppable—except, on that day, by Sarah. South St. Paul, the underdogs, won the game. Although South St. Paul went on to lose a heartbreaker in the semi-finals of the State Tournament, Sarah says of the game against Eagan and Darwitz, "*That* was my State Championship."

At the end of her senior year, Sarah was one of five finalists for Minnesota's All-State Goalie of the Year. She had reached the peak of high school hockey. She was set to graduate, and with graduation, she would have an opportunity to hang up her skates.

But Sarah didn't hang up her skates. It would have been impossible to have done so. She was a goalie; she had to go on being a goalie. That first hour at the Bloomington Ice Garden had been a call that could not be ignored, and the Garden was about to weave an even wilder story with young Sarah. Her father admits he couldn't have foreseen the call of her high school career, so he surely couldn't have seen that of her college career. Sarah was on her way to become the goalie at Princeton University.

There was one goalie ahead of Sarah on the Princeton team, but at a tournament over Thanksgiving, Sarah was given a turn in the net. She shut out Yale and Ohio State. For the rest of her freshman year, she played every minute in the net. In her sophomore year at

Princeton, Sarah was replaced in the net by another goalie. Both father and daughter recalled it as "a time for humility." In the tone of their voices, there is the sense of the *gift* of humility.

After her college career at Princeton, Sarah went on to play for the first women's professional hockey team; she tried out for the Olympic team, and began to coach girls' high school hockey. During the 2005-06 season, she was an assistant coach for South St. Paul High School, her *alma mater*. In that year, they won the State Tournament. Everything had come full circle. Sarah still plays on a Minnesota women's team; she skates in a national tournament in Boston each year; and she says, "I'll be skating until I'm 80 years old, God willing."

"God willing."

When Sarah speaks of hockey, she speaks of the time with her father, and how special it was to have him teach her. She speaks of working with her father on a dream of hers, and a dream of his, and that they could be a team working on the dream. She even speaks of the gift of her parents' marriage, and how her parents met when they were both fourteen years old. It is a great gift to her that they have such an amazing marriage. But the thing that cannot be missed when Sarah speaks of hockey is her love for God.

"All the glory goes to the Lord; that's the main idea. I believe, I have faith in the Lord."

Where did Sarah get her faith? From the witness of her parents, and in a particular way, on that frozen pond in the front yard where her father first taught her.

Although Sarah has been single-hearted in her career as goalie, it doesn't mean she has not suffered losses. Her father knows what makes Sarah great: "She isn't a quitter." Again and again she returns to the net, she is in the game. Heartbreaking losses fade with great victories. Even now, Sarah returns to the memory of her great wins, and to that first hour at the Bloomington Ice Garden whenever she faces difficulties in hockey or in life. "Hockey goes on, the dream goes on, life goes on, and nothing is impossible with God."

✝

We constantly ask our youth if they are ready to be confirmed, but this may be the wrong question. Cal Ahlquist had a different take on it: if Sarah were to be a goalie, she would have to take the shots, all the shots. If hockey is what you want, then this is what you will receive, quiet little angled shots, sharp shots that come in high and low, and blistering, unforgiving slap shots that carry their own lessons in humility. The hour in front of the goal at that miraculous Ice Garden session was Sarah's last chance to get out, to leave hockey. She took everything her father dished out and at the end of the hour was *confirmed* in her choice to be a goalie. She made the life-changing decision to take whatever shots were to come her way. Sarah has been single-hearted in her love for hockey—and in her love for God.

Perhaps we need to ask our youth who are about to be confirmed: "Are you ready to take shots for being a faithful Catholic?" The world is relentless in its attack. Some attacks will come quietly; some will come with sharp angles; and some will be blistering, unforgiving slap shots that bring their own lessons in humility.

Sarah points to her parents' witness as fundamental to her catechesis. Their marriage helped strengthen her zest for hockey and life—and for her faith. Cal spoke of the "raw moves" on the "frozen pond" as somehow better than the teaching of the "classroom," or the ice rink. He understood that the everyday ordinariness of teaching his daughter was essential. We can catechize our children through the everyday ordinary goings on of life. If we don't *flinch* when it comes to following the Church and Her teachings, it is likely that our children won't either.

Do our youth really want "in?" Do they really want to stand in the net and take the shots? Are they *confirmed* in their decision to be Confirmed? Then their catechesis must take on the appropriate weight. Put on the equipment that your Faith provides, get in the net, and prepare to take the shots. In order to become faithful Catholics, our children must have "the uncanny ability to be fearless."

> Then many of his disciples who were listening said, "This saying is
> hard; who can accept it?" Since Jesus knew that his disciples were
> murmuring about this, he said to them, "Does this shock you?"…
> As a result of this, many of his disciples returned to their former
> way of life and no longer accompanied him. Jesus then said to the
> Twelve, "Do you also want to leave?" Simon Peter answered him,
> "Master, to whom shall we go? You have the words of eternal life.
> We have come to believe and are convinced that you are the Holy
> One of God." (John 6:60-61, 66-69)

Chapter Twenty-Two

THE HEART

There is a little prairie town in the northeast corner of South Dakota. When strangers drive through, they may wonder what, if anything, ever happens in the sleepy town. But the residents know that it is a town full of little, or not so little, surprises. In 1999, Aberdeen welcomed Don Meyer as coach to the Northern State University Wolves men's basketball team. By the spring of 2008, after a total of 36 years of coaching college basketball, nine with the Northern Wolves, Meyer had amassed 891 wins, twelve shy of breaking the all-time record for NCAA college men's basketball. The record was certain to be broken in the following season. However, on September 5, 2008, before the new season began, Meyer suffered a near fatal accident when his car was hit by a semi-truck on a country road not far from Aberdeen. While receiving emergency surgery to save his life, doctors discovered that Meyer had cancer. Later, doctors had to amputate a portion of his left leg because of complications from the accident. When Meyer was awake and able to communicate, he wrote on a piece of paper, "How long before I can coach?"[12]

What followed was a journey of pain, fortitude, virtue, self-sacrifice, and love. A former player of Coach Meyer recalls his teaching, "The measurement of a man is his response to adversity."[13] Meyer

---

[12] Buster Olney, *How Lucky You Can Be* (New York: Ballentine Books, 2010) 10, 37-39, 64-65.
[13] Ibid 27.

was about to illustrate this in his journey to return to the basketball court. In a statement to the press, Meyer said:

> What's great about this is I would not have known about the cancer had I not had the wreck. God has blessed me with the one thing we all need, which is truth. I can now fight with all of my ability. What I now ask is that everybody who believes in God would praise Him for this discovery and pray to Him to give me strength, patience, and peace to be a man of God on this journey.[14]

In his coaching career, Meyer was never known as a pushover. He was known for inflicting exhaustion and pain. It was his technique to get the players to ignore outside influences including the crowd and the score. He instilled a sort of fear in his players; they had a fear of *Meyer*, thereby being less distracted by the intangibles of a given game.[15]

There was a day when Meyer angrily told his team, "Just start running!" His team sprinted back and forth on the court. The whole time Meyer yelled at them about their responsibilities to the school and to the team. After 45 minutes, Meyer told them that one of the team had skipped an English class. "A selfish decision by one of them reflected on all of them."[16]

At first glance, it may seem that Meyer would be lucky to have any players at all, let alone be considered one of the greats. It would seem that the players would look for a way to be free of him after playing for him. But that just wasn't the case. While Meyer was in the hospital after the accident, his former players maintained a schedule of visiting him in the hospital. The boys who came to him in college became men under his tutelage. Now they lived out what they had been taught by Coach Meyer, "If you want to be happy in life, you'd better learn to serve others."[17]

[14] Ibid 82.

[15] Ibid 23.

[16] Ibid 13-15.

[17] Ibid 72.

But all this suffering and service for a sport was done for college players. Do we really ask our children to suffer?

$$+$$

As Catholics, we have become accustomed to suffering. Now, when I say *accustomed to*, in this day and age, I mean accustomed to it in the sense of our Catholic humor and the idea of "offering it up." But the world around us has had a great influence here, and we often forego the real offering it up, instead turning from the suffering in front of us to the comforts of the world. Would we ever do this in hockey?

It seems that there have been some concessions in hockey to worldly comfort. In my neck of the woods, there are nearly no leagues that play on outdoor rinks anymore. The ice arenas may still be very cold, but there is no icy wind and skaters and parents no longer worry about frostbite. But does this make hockey devoid of suffering? Of course not.

It can't be all that hard to make a case for skaters suffering in hockey. Being checked into the boards may qualify as suffering. Doing the dreaded *Herbies* certainly qualifies as suffering. Imagine the drilling that teenaged skaters undergo in one season of hockey. They have tired muscles. Their muscles and brains are telling them, "No more, not a second more!" But the drilling continues. They submit to long practices and a huge time commitment. There is competition for positions, not just at the beginning of the season, but throughout the season. There are losing streaks, sometimes long losing streaks. Everything is accompanied by more practices and more drilling.

Hockey skaters, even young hockey skaters, suffer for their sport. Yet, the suffering for the sport doesn't seem to break the souls of the skaters: it seems to elevate the souls of the skaters. There is great satisfaction in having *left everything on the ice.*

When the skater gets into the car after practice, the parent asks, "How was practice?"

The skater replies in utter exhaustion, "Coach was so hard on us."

And the parent, "Good, that's good for you. You are lucky to have a coach who cares so much."

But is it only the skater who suffers for hockey? Imagine being the parent of a skater who cannot yet drive. Someone has to get the child to the 6 a.m. practice on a Saturday. What about the 10 p.m. ice-time on a weeknight? And who has to wake that skater up in the morning to get to school? There are tournaments that consume the weekend.

How about tithing? The money that you have given to hockey was just for the regular season. This tournament was one the team qualified for during the season; write a check. But, it's not just you and the skater going to the tournament, the family is going; hockey is a family event. "Yes, get in the car, we are going as a *family* to see your sister skate." There must now be money for the hotel, gas, and food for the family. Extra money is always needed throughout the season. There is continuous skate sharpening. One stick is not enough; there is broken stick after broken stick that needs replacement, as do the outgrown pads. Teamwear isn't free, and there is the gas to the next rink.

Speaking of the car and suffering, if you have skaters in their early teens, there is a chance that they do not have full access to the locker rooms—so they don't shower after practice or games. They are sweaty after the game and decide to run in the sub-zero temperatures without a coat in order to get to the car. Once in the car, they are freezing, and they request, "Can you turn up the heat?" Yep—now you are suffering for hockey.

Speaking of things that don't exactly smell like roses, let's talk about hockey pads. Unlike summer sports, you cannot make your children leave their sports equipment in the garage. Hockey pads are wet after games. They need to dry out, which can't happen in the frozen garage or car. Not only are wet pads uncomfortable when the skater next wears them, but also, not drying the pads will tend to destroy them sooner. So if you want to talk about suffering for hockey, imagine being at a tournament in a small hotel room and having the pads dry out under your nose as you sleep. "Offer it up!"

+

Is the suffering in hockey redemptive? Yes. Not only does the skater suffer for the good of self, but also, and perhaps more importantly, for the good of the team. In addition, the family suffers for hockey. When the skater makes a commitment, the parents have also made a commitment. The parents join their suffering to the universal good of the team—even the universal good of hockey.

Occasionally, if you listen, you will hear tired parents talking as they wait for the next game, sometimes joined by parents from opposing teams. They will commiserate and share their suffering, and then *offer it up* by saying, "Someday, when the kids are playing with the Gophers, it will all be worth it." The parents see how this suffering now is for the greater good. They see the promise of the future. Although parents know that while many skaters are called to play Gopher hockey, few are chosen. But there is still this sense of the possible. All of the long hours, the broken sticks, the early mornings and late nights, the skate sharpening, the tired muscles, the defeats, the tithing, all of this will be worth it when the parent can state, "My child skates for the Gophers." Many are called, few are chosen, but the hope is strong.

What if the child never skates for the Gophers? Is the suffering worth it? When the skater comes to the car worn out and stinking, it was worth having left everything on the ice. Later that night, when the parents see the skater sleeping deeply, the suffering of the day was worth it. The parents are witnessing a child who *offered up* suffering for hockey success. The parents now know that they too must offer up today's suffering for the glory of hockey, which is for the good of their child—even if he or she never makes it to the Gophers—or even to the high school team. The parent instinctively knows that the child will take the lessons of hockey and teamwork throughout the rest of his or her life. Even this day was worth it. Offer it up.

✝

So what happened in the little prairie town of Aberdeen, South Dakota? Did Coach Meyer ever return to coach the Northern Wolves? Did he break the record? Or, did he, understandably, retire, leaving the record for someone else?

Meyer was in a wheelchair at his first practice, his voice weak, but he was back to coach his team. By January 2009, Meyer was one game from breaking the record for winningest NCAA men's college basketball coach. Meyer had a tradition of letting special guests at games sit on the Wolves bench. There were many special guests in attendance that evening when the record might be broken. On the bench that night were Don Carda and his wife, Reva. Don had driven the semi-truck that hit Meyer's car just a few months earlier.[18] In everything Meyer lived his own advice, "The measurement of a man is his response to adversity."

With just under five minutes left in the game, the crowd began to chant, "Nine-Oh-Three... Nine-Oh-Three," which was about to become the number of wins Meyer had achieved.[19] Just minutes later it was official, Coach Don Meyer had become the winningest NCAA men's college basketball coach of all time.

In a speech after the game, Meyer said:

> We're never going to be able to thank all of you. But you need to know how much it means to us. And you need to keep praying for the leg to recover and the cancer maybe to go away. But most of all you need to pray that we all keep the spirit you all have exhibited toward our family and our team.[20]

[18] Ibid 147.

[19] Ibid 147.

[20] Ibid 148.

Meyer, although not born in Aberdeen, has become a favorite son of Aberdeen. He challenged his players to always be ready. "When you get your chance, you've got to raise the level of intensity. You've got to raise the level of confidence. You've got to raise the level of excellence."[21] In essence, by pushing his teams to suffer, to work, to execute, he called them to offer it up and put their hearts into it. His teams responded with an emphatic, "Yes!" By calling his players to greatness, he called the small prairie town to greatness, and in a way, he calls us all to greatness.

Later, when receiving the *Jimmy V. Award*, from ESPN, Meyer said of his incredible journey, "I've learned from this odyssey that peace is not the absence of troubles, trials, and torment, but calm in the midst of them."[22] Ah, yes, this is a man who understands suffering; he understands the journey, not just of basketball, but of *life*.

+

Jenna and her family knew Mass times all over town. They made a commitment to hockey, but knew that their commitment to the Faith took precedence. As a family, they decided to offer up any games that kept them from Mass. It was the Saturday evening before Sunday's third place game in the tournament, and the coach announced the time of the big game to his skaters. Eleven-year-old Jenna replied, "Coach, that's not going to work for me. We checked the Mass schedule; there are two Masses and they both overlap with the game."

Her coach made a strong case when he said, "Jenna, I think God will understand. You can go twice next week."

Without hesitation, the child calmly replied, "I think God will understand that I chose hockey instead of Him."

Hockey instead of Him—the choice has been made countless times, but not by Jenna. She knew that the choice always must be Him instead of Hockey. So she *offered up* hockey.

---

[21] Ibid 206.

[22] Ibid 188.

Jenna joined her family at Mass. The third place game was still underway upon their return to the rink. Uniform on, she joined her teammates on the ice. Her team won, but the real victory came when the coach told her, "You taught me something today."

Jenna was calm and prepared. Offering up her beloved hockey wasn't painless. But she still made the act of the will, a decision she had made from the beginning of the season.

+

In hockey, families will sacrifice physically, spiritually, and financially. Skaters at every age are expected to sacrifice physically and spiritually. They are to submit to the practices and the games, and all the drilling that accompanies them. We call our children to a full physical and spiritual involvement in hockey from the youngest age. However, we rarely do the same in the Faith. Even the youngest child will rise to the challenge of physical and spiritual sacrifice for hockey. What if we were to ask them—even just strongly encourage them—to do this for the Faith?

From the stands, in hockey, we will cheer skaters on by asking them to *put their hearts into it*. We do this especially when the going is tough. It is implicit in our cheering that *putting your heart into it* is an *act of the will*. By cheering in this manner, we imply that the skater has a choice, to skate with "no heart", or to dig deeply and to skate with a heart full of expectation and desire. Putting your heart into it is an act of the will. In hockey, we admit it, we call for it, and we expect that the skater's heart is to be fully engaged.

We rarely ask our children to physically and spiritually sacrifice when it comes to the Faith. This is exactly why *offering it up* has been relegated to a type of Catholic humor. Yet, suffering for the Faith doesn't break the souls of our youth, it elevates them. There is a great satisfaction in having *given everything*—putting the heart into it. When our youth learn to serve, to really offer up, to be Christ to others, they experience a new sort of victory.

What if at the Mass, we leaned over and encouraged our children to *put their hearts into it?* In fact, God does ask this of *all* of us, young and old. "Lift up your *hearts!*"

Is our response just tired and rote? Or is it full and beautiful, with expectation and desire?

"Lift up your *hearts!*"

"We lift them up to the Lord!"

Chapter Twenty-Three

THE STANLEY CUP

"What is the ultimate reward in hockey?"

Usually when I ask this question, there are a few answers from the audience, ranging from a state high school championship, to a college championship, to the gold medal, and the Stanley Cup. However, when I ask it again, with emphasis added, "What is the *ultimate* reward in hockey?" The answers narrow to just one, the Stanley Cup. I'll ask, "What about the other rewards you mentioned?" Explanations vary, but usually have something to do with having not heard me correctly, but now knowing that I was looking for the ultimate reward, the Stanley Cup is the only answer.

Pushing the audience further, I ask for dissenting voices, "Surely, there must be some dissenting voices." There are none, ever. I ask everyone who has already spoken to hold their thoughts and then ask the shy people in the audience to voice their opinions. There is usually a pause, and then someone quietly says, "The Stanley Cup."

"Okay, so we agree, with no dissenting voices, that the Stanley Cup is the *ultimate* reward in hockey.... This seems too easy; there is almost never a time when all adults believe exactly the same thing. What I need you to do is to really examine the question and then tell me, what is the *ultimate* reward in hockey?"

After a pause, I ask again for the *ultimate* reward in hockey. Still the audience only has one answer and by now they seem just the tiniest bit perturbed that I keep asking. They answer, "The Stanley Cup."

"Last chance for dissenting voices.… Then it looks like everyone is in agreement, with no dissenting voices, we can proclaim that the Stanley Cup is the *ultimate* reward in hockey!"

There are more nods from the audience.

"Great! It has been decided, the Stanley Cup is the *ultimate* reward in hockey…and it is not available to your daughters."

Then the gasp.

Slowly this time, "Yes, the Stanley Cup *is* the ultimate reward in hockey and it is not available to your daughters. Only your sons can dream of the Stanley Cup."

Of course there are many wonderful rewards in hockey for women and girls, but none is the Stanley Cup. We have all admitted it. I searched for dissenting voices. There were none. There is no going back.

+

One evening, while sharing a meal with my cousin, Dominic pointed out that there might be one day when a woman could become a goalie in the NHL and potentially win the Stanley Cup. "Ah—great, let's look at who the Stanley Cup is available to."

Could a woman goalie really win the Cup? Could a woman goalie actually sustain the pounding she would take in the net during the season from the male skaters? There has never even been a woman who skated a single regular season game in the NHL, much less won the Cup. If we are honest with ourselves, the Stanley Cup is not only not available to our daughters, but also, it is not available to all of our sons. If you have a son with Down's syndrome, the Stanley Cup is not available to him. If you have a son who has physical handicaps, the Stanley Cup is not available to him. A case could even be made for boys who only reach 5' of height, or those over 7' tall; the Stanley Cup is most likely not available to them. What about your son without vision in one eye? What about your son who was catechized in hockey at the age of 25? It is highly unlikely that he would win a Stanley Cup.

The Stanley Cup is only available to an *elite* group of *men!*

✝

Let me say it again: the Stanley Cup is only available to an *elite* group of *men!*

These are men with *exceptional* physical prowess. But it is not just physical prowess. The prowess must be harnessed. These men have *exceptional* discipline. They have put in a lifetime of work to reach the level of winning a Stanley Cup. Oddly, I have never heard anyone complain about the Stanley Cup only being open to an elite group of men.

In fact there is something glorious about watching this elite group of men exercise their exceptional physical prowess knowing that it is backed by exceptional discipline as they skate toward an award that has never been open to me. Somehow, I am able to join their dream as a fan. Their glory takes nothing from me. Instead, I would argue, that being a fan is to have a share in the full glory; the team is acting on my behalf. In essence, if my team wins, I too am a winner. Although I will never be the actual Stanley Cup winner, if the Minnesota Wild win the Cup, I would then gladly exclaim, "*We* won the Stanley Cup!" Forever, I will only be a fan, but I'll never feel left out of the glory of what is happening in front of me on the ice; the sacrifice of the game and the victory of the Stanley Cup.

As a side note, the *ultimate* reward in the Church is *not* the priesthood; it is the Eternal Crown of Glory—but more on that later.

Back to the Stanley Cup—no one, or more correctly, no *man* wins the Stanley Cup after having only just strapped on a pair of skates. In essence, no man gains the Cup without having put in years of preparation; a lifetime of work goes into winning it.

Upon winning the Cup, the man receives a particular honor. He gets to spend 24 hours with the actual Stanley Cup. He could have a parade with the Cup. He could have a picnic with the Cup. He might take the Cup to the local rink where he started skating, as a symbol of the journey. He can take the cup *anywhere* in that 24 hours. There are even a couple of babies who have been baptized in the cup! However, if you do win the Cup and want your baby baptized in it, I would suggest checking with your priest before sending out the Stanley Cup Baptismal invitations for Junior; there is the *slimmest* chance that Father would rather use the font in church than the Stanley Cup.

But the point is really that the man who wins the Cup gets 24 hours with it before giving it back. If he had such a great time with the Cup, and would like another 24 hours, it's simple; he just has to win it again! This may not be so far-fetched; there are men who have won the Cup multiple times. Henri Richard has won the Cup 11 times; that's 11 days with the Cup. Jean Beliveau and Yvan Cournoyer both won the Cup 10 times; that's 10 days each with the Cup. Of course, after each 24-hour period of time, the Cup is returned.

How many boys and men have dreamt of the Cup but never won it? Many are called and few are chosen. How many boys have never made it past the junior high team? Or the high school team? Or the college team? How many professional skaters have never won the Cup? "For many are called, but few are chosen." (Matthew 22:14)[23]

We don't say of these men and boys, "They should have stuck to stamp collecting." "What a waste of a life." "What a wasted effort." No, instead, there is glory in the effort—even if they never receive the Cup. The effort was heroic and valiant and glorious in itself. Many are called, but few are chosen for the Stanley Cup.

The priesthood, like the Stanley Cup, is only open to men. This is not to say a *perfect* group of men, but it is an elite group. In hockey, the team acts on behalf of the fans, taking nothing away from the

---

[23] *The Holy Bible*, Revised Standard Version (San Francisco: Ignatius Press, 1966)

fans, instead giving to them. In the Mass, the priest acts on behalf of the congregation, taking nothing away from them, instead giving to them. Also, like the Stanley Cup, the priesthood is not open to all men. A Down's syndrome boy will not become a priest. A man with a very low mental capacity will not become a priest. Although there are exceptions, men who are married are not able to become priests. The priesthood, like the Stanley Cup, is only open to an elite group of men. Many are called; few are chosen.

But the priesthood is *not* the ultimate reward in the Church—the Eternal Crown of Glory is! The eternal crown of glory is open to our sons and *daughters*. It is given to us when we meet our Maker. We are confronted with our lives and hope to hear, "Well done, my good and faithful servant." (Matthew 25:23) If we hear this, we are given a crown—an *eternal* crown of glory. It is not for just 24 hours. It does not have to be won over and over again. It is given once, for all eternity, and never taken away.

The eternal crown of glory is available to *all* of our sons and daughters. It is available to children with and without physical or mental prowess. It is available to those with physical and mental handicaps—perhaps, in a sense, it's even more available to them.

It is a great glory in hockey when our sons seek its ultimate reward, the Stanley Cup. This glory is amplified upon winning the Cup.

It is a greater glory when our sons and daughters seek their final reward, the Eternal Crown of Glory. This glory is amplified upon being given the crown.

"'Come,' says my heart, 'seek God's face'; your face, Lord, do I seek!" (Psalms 27:8)

Chapter Twenty-Four

THE EFFORT

We often hear the word "martyr." It seems it must mean some kind of bloody death. When we ask our children whether they would like to be martyrs, the usual answer is that they don't want to be—although there are a few exceptions as a child fakes a gruesome ending. But what is this word "martyr?" It is a Greek word and it means "witness." In Hebrew it also means "witness," but one of the lesser meanings in Hebrew is "a repeated action," like a hammer hitting metal over and over again.

This repeated action is a witness as well. Imagine the hammer hitting metal day-in and day-out, in season and out of season, continuously hitting the metal. At times this action may amount to tedium, but if the hammer's *job* is to hit the metal repeatedly, then the hammer is faithful in carrying out its job. As Catholics, we are called to this same sort of faith. We must live our faith, follow the Church teachings, in season and out of season.

As an example, let's look to St. Peter Martyr. His name gives away his manner of death: martyrdom. It was a bloody finish. Let me say it in a different way: Peter Martyr was called to the glorious death of a *witness*, for from the time of his conversion, Peter Martyr lived the *repeated actions* of his faith, in season and out of season. A case could be made that the repeated actions of faith in his life made him *able* to suffer as he did. In his final moments, he could have renounced his faith. Instead, the repeated actions of his life of faith allowed him to *put on Christ,* so in the end, there was only Christ. The day in, day out, everyday ordinariness of his life of faith prepared him for the Eternal Crown of Glory.

+

Great hockey is not born of spasms of activity whenever skaters want to play the game. Instead, it takes constant exercise and effort. Imagine the effort that goes into winning the Stanley Cup, the repeated falls, the hard hits on the ice, the injuries. Imagine the drilling, the years and years of drilling that quickly become tedium and continue to the point of utter exhaustion and then past exhaustion. Drilling and practices amount to years and years of repeated actions in which a skater *puts on hockey.* In hockey it is *expected* that this will be the case; it is expected by the skaters, the coach, the parents, the fans. Everyone understands that the repeated action of drilling and practice is the only way to hone skills and become a *martyr* or *witness* for hockey. It is a dedication expected from the youngest skater to the professional.

A complaint of many parents who have students in religious education is that the child is only learning the same thing year after year. The parents see no reason to continue to bring their children back year after year, they see no reason for the repeated actions of the teaching.

Interestingly, in hockey there has seemingly never been a coach at any level, including the professional level, who hasn't said, "We must get back to basics." What are the youngest skaters learning? They are learning to skate forward and backward and side-to-side. They are learning to shoot the puck, receive the puck, and to pass the puck. They are learning the rules, their positions, and how to play as a team.

What are the professional skaters learning? They are learning to skate forward and backward and side-to-side. They are learning to shoot the puck, receive the puck, and to pass the puck. They are learning the rules, their positions, and to play as a team. But the professionals are learning to do all of this *at a much deeper level!*

In a certain sense, the discipline of hockey is quite simple. Of course, at another level, the discipline of hockey is *deep* and somehow even *mystical*. The young skaters are just *learning* to put on hockey—but they haven't yet achieved this. The professionals *have* put on hockey—and the way their status is maintained is by the repeated action of drilling and practice.

One of my favorite plays in all of sports occurs in baseball, especially professional baseball. Professional pitchers have the fastest fastballs, which makes this play all the more impressive. The event takes only seconds. The pitcher throws a hard ball at nearly 100 miles per hour to the hitter, the hitter then takes a wooden bat and pounds the hard ball right back at the pitcher, the speed of the ball now greatly increased because of the force of the bat. *If* a non-pitcher happened to be standing on the mound, every good sense would tell that non-pitcher to duck and cover. However, an actual pitcher only flinches a bit, but the flinch has nothing to do with duck and cover—instead the flinch is his catching hand going out from his body and catching the *bullet* coming back at him.

How is a pitcher able to do this? Simple, he has *put on baseball.* The professional pitcher has honed his skills over years by repeated actions of drilling and practice. He has *put on baseball* so in that moment there is only *baseball.* The *flinch* that catches the ball is a flinch of discipline born of repeated training—or, in a sense, *martyrdom.*

Years of practice and the tedium of drilling are necessary to put on hockey, or baseball, or even the Faith.

An interesting phenomenon takes place in the Faith. The second grade religious education classes usually have two to four times the amount of students that the third grade religious education classes have. Later, in ninth grade, religious education classes jump back to the second grade levels, but completely disappear the following year.

What is this phenomenon about? The Sacramental years. In second grade the child receives both First Reconciliation and First Communion. Then in ninth grade, or thereabouts, youth receive Confirmation. The parents feel justified in removing their children after second grade, with the excuse that the children are just learning the same thing over and over in future years. The Faith may or may not be supported at home during these years when the child is absent from classes; this time can be a fertile season for loss of a child's Faith.

We never hear of such a phenomenon in hockey. Never do we hear of parents who have their children skate through second grade, pull them out of hockey all together, then bring them back to hockey in ninth grade and expect them to skate on the high school team. If there were such parents we would be shocked by the boldness of their presumption. All of hockey would rightfully exclaim, "Are you kidding? Good luck with that!" Skaters are expected to be *faithful* to hockey throughout the years. Why? So they may best *put on hockey*, they are to be martyrs, witnesses, of hockey through the years, in season and out of season. Someone with the skill set of a second grader, moreover, is not prepared to be on the ice with those who have been faithful to hockey through the years. Their lack of repeated drilling and practice leave them at a great disadvantage for being on the ice with skaters who are far advanced.

Remember my friend Melissa and her skating family? Let me clarify one thing. She has two sons, but only one has ever played hockey. Jake played hockey since he was a very young boy. Ryan was not interested in hockey when he was very young; he came to hockey later. When that time came, Melissa and Mike looked to find a team for Ryan. However they were told that Ryan had waited too long, he was too old to begin hockey. Ryan was just nine years old.

In hockey there is an *expectation* that skaters will come to the ice at a young age, remain faithful, and be a martyr, a witness to hockey, repeating the actions of drilling and practice, in order to best *put on hockey*. The professionals have *put on hockey*. Hearing a professional speak of a game where everything was coming together at once, everything firing correctly, is to hear of a near mystical experience. The professionals speak about having skated in a manner that is almost beyond themselves, of having been outside of time—in some kind of slow motion that happens in the blink of an eye. *All* the years of drilling and practice, their whole body of knowledge of hockey, had come together in one moment. They are hockey's *martyrs*; at that moment, there is only *hockey* left.

However, every game is not a spiritual experience for even the greatest skater. Every practice is not a joy and every new set of drills seems to offer no promise except exhaustion. Hockey can be a chore; hockey is difficult. Some days even the professional skater is dragging himself to the rink. But the greats show up. The greats go through another, seemingly endless day of the repeated actions of drilling and practicing. Some games, even for the greats, are a seeming exercise in futility. But the greats show up for the repeated actions in order to put on hockey and to become a witness.

The *greats* can be of any age. They may be just learning to stand on skates or they may have won multiple Cups. But the greats have made a commitment and show up for the everyday, ordinary goings on of playing hockey. They put on hockey in season and out of season. And then there is the day that happens at every age level, that day when time stops and the skater skates outside of himself, and skating becomes mystical.

Skating is an act of the will, especially on days when the body would rather not be dragged onto the ice. Skating is a choice. To skate, or not to skate, that is the question. Hockey skaters have made a choice to be on a team, they have a commitment to the team. Hockey is not just between the skater and the commissioner. Skating is a commitment to a community. Skating is not based on feelings; it is an act of the will. But to have that feeling, even once, that mystical out-of-body feeling, is rather extraordinary.

Being faithful is an act of the will. As Catholics, our faith is not just "Me and Jesus." Our commitment is to the whole mystical body.

Every day of being faithful is not always a great joy. Being at Mass is not always a mystical experience. Prayer can very often be dry. The everyday, ordinary goings on of being faithful are not about *feelings*. Instead faith is an act of the will. However, to have that feeling, even once, that mystical out-of-body feeling, is rather extraordinary.

Imagine the effort then that goes into winning that Stanley Cup. There are years and years of drilling and practice. Physical and spiritual exhaustion are constant companions. There are injuries, sacrifice, and unbelievable discipline. Is it all worth it in the end? Once you have won the Stanley Cup, the hundreds of broken sticks mean nothing. The missing teeth only make your smile bigger and the blood looks good on your uniform. You have the Cup and the effort was *nothing*.

If this is the kind of effort that goes into winning a Stanley Cup, imagine the effort that should go into winning the Eternal Crown of Glory! It may entail years of drilling, physical and spiritual exhaustion, sacrifices, discipline—possibly even injuries to spirit and body. It *will* be worth it in the end! Once you have the Eternal Crown of Glory, the hours of catechism at home and at the parish appear all the more precious. The hard knocks of being faithful make the crown more glorious. Even the blood of the martyrs serves to enhance the crown. You will have the crown and the effort will have been worth it.

We mentioned before that there is glory in the effort of those who will never win the Cup. Their effort will have been its own glory. But if they have never won the Stanley Cup, they will *never* have those 24 hours with the Cup.

Effort will be rewarded; the soul may have to go through a purgation, but *glorious* effort will not be ignored. The crown may still be given, given for eternity.

We would never advise someone to wait to the last minute to win the Cup. The effort for the Cup must be life-long. The usual path to the Crown is sustained effort, time and effort and discipline—and getting up after hitting the "ice."

There is only one thing any of us really wants to hear at the end of our lives: "Well done, good and faithful servant." There is only *one* ultimate reward in the Church: the Eternal Crown of Glory.

Do you not know that the runners in the stadium all run in the race, but only one wins the prize? Run so as to win. Every athlete exercises discipline in every way. They do it to win a perishable crown, but we an imperishable one. (1 Corinthians 9:24-25)

Chapter Twenty-Five

WINNING THE CUP

There was a particular day when the grade school principal called to ask me to substitute teach the following day. "Sure, I'm available. What class?" Her reply, "Gym." There was a groan, a chortle, and then that certain sort of resignation, knowing that I already said I was available and that she must be desperate if she were calling me. "Yes, I'll be there." Being a great principal, she didn't exactly wait around on the phone while I changed my mind. "Great, I'll see you tomorrow," she said.

To the best of my recollection, my last foray into gym class included an old phonograph playing a scratchy record of *Go You Chicken Fat, Go!* I had no idea what I was going to do with the kids. But then it came to me; I could do research for *The Catechism of Hockey*. There I was in the gym with about 20 seventh and eighth grade girls looking at me. When they heard about doing research for a book, there was cheering, hugging, and a general excitement.

The first thing was to ask them what the ultimate reward is in hockey. There was no hesitation; instead there was a competition to say it first. The girls ran the words together as they proclaimed, "TheStanleyCup!" It was fantastic; to a girl, they each understood the Stanley Cup to be the ultimate reward. Then I sprung it on them, "You're right. The Stanley Cup is the ultimate reward, but it's not available to girls." What I expected next was disappointment, as though I had tricked them. But there was no disappointment; there was only that sort of noncommittal, "Mhmm." Already, the research was great. This group of all teenaged girls didn't care at all that the Stanley Cup was only available to men. Not one even had an inclination to discuss it. They were ready to get to the next part.

I set the scene. "For our research today, we will pretend that I am training you to win the Cup." We picked out a Stanley Cup stand-in; it was a stick horse someone had found in a forgotten corner of the gymnasium closet. "Alright, we are going to practice winning the Cup." There was a moment of silence, and then I announced, "Ladies and gentlemen, I am proud to present your 2011 Stanley Cup winners!" There was cheering and jumping around from the girls as they took hold of the stick horse. Then they suddenly stopped and looked at me.

"Tell me what you think."

They looked at me with an odd sort of stare. So I said, "Okay, let's practice winning the Cup again." Once again, I announced, "Ladies and gentlemen, I am proud to present your 2011 Stanley Cup winners!" There was jumping and cheering again; again they reached for the stick horse; again they quickly stopped and stared at me.

"Now what happened?"

One of the girls said, "We're not going to win it."

"Why not?"

Another girl: "We aren't practicing."

"Sure you are, you're practicing winning the Cup."

"That's not how you win the Cup."

"What do you mean?"

Then the other girls in rapid succession said, "You have to practice." "We haven't learned anything." "You haven't taught us to skate." "We can't win without doing anything."

Pretending not to understand them, I again used that assuring tone, "Well then, let's try it again. We will practice winning the Cup." And again, "Ladies and gentlemen, I'm proud to present your 2011 Stanley Cup winners."

There was a little half-hearted cheering this time, in conjunction with a few hops, and a couple of girls holding the ridiculous Stanley-Cup-stand-in, the horse on a stick. This was accompanied by that dead stare of exasperated teenagers. But what followed was breathtakingly beautiful: no mystic could have said it better, the single voice in the background, in that loud disdainful are-you-kidding-me tone, flatly said, "It's fake."

Of course, my response was, "Fantastic!" And then, "Tell me what you're thinking."

There were girls' voices coming from all over. "You don't practice getting the trophy." "We didn't do anything." "We would never win by just practicing getting handed the Cup." "That's not how it's done." "It isn't any fun if you didn't work for it." This accompanied by the multiple repetitions of, "Yeah, it's fake!"

Continuing to test them, I said, "But wouldn't this be the best way? If you want to win the Cup, shouldn't you practice the actual winning of the Cup?"

More answers in rapid succession, "Winning takes work, a lot of work." "You have to actually practice the skating, we need to know hockey."

"But doesn't it make sense to practice winning the cup, being handed the cup? Shouldn't we maybe even work on taking team pictures and signing autographs? Won't everyone want your autograph?"

"That's the easy part, you'll just know how to do it. To win you have to practice skating, practice hockey."

"Ah, do you mean that the actual moment of winning the Cup will come naturally?"

All the girls in unison, "Yes."

"So you don't need to practice what will come naturally?"

Again in unison, "No."

"Why not?"

"It will just be that great and you won't be able to help being excited. You'll just know."

"Ah, yes, fantastic. You've taught me just what I wanted to know. Now what would you like to do for gym class?" They played capture the flag, basketball, and volleyball and were happy that I didn't make them do calisthenics. My research was done and the girls were a great gift.

✝

Later, after having told a friend the story, she said, "But what does practicing winning the Cup have to do with faith?"

"Marriage."

"What do you mean?"

Today, it is nearly expected that couples will live together before being married, or at the very least, sleep together before marriage. The excuse is most often that the couple is seeing if they are compatible. Especially if a couple lives together before marriage, they excuse it with *practicing marriage*, because if they don't get this part right then the marriage won't work. It seems good on paper, but the statistics just don't bear out this line of reasoning.

Oddly, the couples that don't live together and don't even sleep together before being married are seen as possibly uninformed, or crazy, or even seen as being blind to the obvious. They are often pressured by others *to* sleep together. They are told by the world that their marriage will never work if they don't know if they are compatible.

It seems that when the world says "compatible in marriage," they really mean "compatible in bed," and give little or no thought to being compatible in marriage. Of course not living or sleeping together before marriage is not a guarantee of success, but the until-death-do-you-part section has a substantially better chance.

So what is with these chaste couples? Simply, they practice the difficult parts of marriage before the actual marriage. It's not that they don't desire each other physically, but they practice a different form of compatibility. Is this someone for whom I can sacrifice?

Chaste couples sacrifice for each other; they delay gratification of the physical, and instead delve into the hard work and sacrifice of discovering true compatibility. They actually spend their time communicating! It's wild, I know, but they talk. Throughout this whole "conversation" of dating and being engaged, they still have the same physical urges as every other couple throughout history. However, they remained focused on the vow that looms in the distance. Can they make the day-in day-out *choice*, the act of the will, of loving each other until death?

The other thing that chaste couples seem to do quite a bit is pray together! I've seen things as radical as chaste couples accompanying each other to Mass! And that's not all—to Adoration as well—praying the rosary together—even volunteering together. I could go on, but I hate to say more unless I know you are sitting down.

Are you sure that's a sturdy chair? All right, here is another thing chaste couples don't do...they don't live together *even when it would make financial sense for them to do so!* (How's your heart? Are you okay?) Oddly enough, tying yourselves together financially before you tie yourselves together spiritually in marriage is nearly always fatal to the marriage.

Of course, I could go on and on, but your pallor isn't exactly rosy. What it boils down to for chaste couples is *sacrifice*. They *do* practice marriage. But instead of practicing the part that comes naturally, they practice the part that has to do with the hard work of the Cross.

+

Who knew hockey was so similar to marriage? Couples that live together before marriage may give the excuse that they are *practicing* marriage. But they are only practicing the part that comes naturally. In essence, they practice *receiving the Cup* without *learning how to skate*. They want the *Cup...now!* The true sacrifice of waiting is foreign to them. They have practiced the big reward over and over. But in the immortal words of a junior high school girl, "It's fake."

Ah, but those poor couples that wait until marriage, how will they know what to do?

It was another wise junior high school girl who said, "That's the easy part, you'll just know how to do it." It seems she's right. Of all the couples I've known who have waited, I've never even heard a rumor about a couple that didn't have it all figured out by morning.

You cannot win the Cup without sacrifice. You cannot be married without sacrifice. Marriage begins at the Altar. Everyone forgets that the Altar is a place of sacrifice. You cannot celebrate the joy of winning the Cup unless there is first great sacrifice. You cannot celebrate the joy of marriage without making all of the necessary sacrifice.

Chapter Twenty-Six

SAFE HOCKEY

Hockey is beautiful, and hockey is dangerous. Considering the danger, it is a wonder that we let our children play it at all. Even on the first day, or perhaps, especially on the first day, our children will get hurt as they learn to skate. At some time, our children will meet the cold hard ice, and often in a dramatic way.

Football is beautiful, and football is dangerous. Soccer is beautiful and dangerous, as are baseball, and biking, and horseback riding, and ballet, and cheerleading, and gymnastics, and so many of the other activities in which our children participate. In addition to these, I posit that something like the piano or the cello is beautiful *and* dangerous.

Wow! You've made it through twenty-five chapters and now the crazy woman writing this wants you to believe that piano is dangerous. I admit that you have made a remarkable commitment to reading *The Catechism of Hockey*, and you are so close to the end; it would be a shame to have to quit now. So, let me make my case before you close the book, and take it to the St. Vincent de Paul thrift store.

Piano *is* dangerous. Why? There is a little thing called passion, and passion is beautiful, but it has a taste of danger in it as well. Passion involves a commitment of the heart, and investment of the soul. Anytime the heart and soul are involved in anything, there is a certain danger. The level of danger varies depending on the level of commitment and investment of the heart and soul.

When your child is learning where middle *C* is on a piano key-board, there is most likely no danger. Scales have little or no danger in them...until you hear someone play scales with *passion*. And, if you have the opportunity to hear someone play it, you cannot miss the danger in Beethoven's *Thunderstorm* from Symphony Six. There is even a certain sort of danger in his romantic *Moonlight Sonata*.

Think of two different people playing the *Moonlight Sonata*, one a young student, the second a virtuoso. When the young student plays it, it may be beautiful in that sweet sort of way. The child has advanced well beyond finding middle *C*, having discovered where all the notes are, and the how-tos of timing bars of music. It is a delight for the parents and grandparents to hear. But there is some-thing remarkably different when the virtuoso plays the *Moonlight Sonata*. Somehow the virtuoso has *lost* herself in the music. It is no longer just the *rules* of piano, knowing the notes in the correct order. Instead, now it is deeply *music*. Her heart and soul are, in a sense, exposed in the music. And that sort of vulnerability can be one of the most dangerous things. Somehow, from within the rules of piano, the virtuoso has moved to a deep, spiritual level; there is a certain *oneness* between the pianist and the piano. When we hear her, we cannot help but to be *involved*. There is some part of our heart that recognizes both the beauty and the *danger*. It's riveting. The beauty is no longer the sweetness of youth, but now holds the mature beauty and danger of passion.

Hockey is no different. There is a certain sweet beauty in seeing four- and five-year-olds out on the ice. Nothing is cuter than watch-ing them skate in a clump, not exactly knowing where the puck is, tripping over their own feet and skates, and at times putting the puck in the wrong net. To be a spectator at these games is to be relaxed, chuckling from time to time, cheering in an encouraging manner, and probably casually chatting with other parents during the play of the game.

Fast-forward ten years, when some of the same children begin to skate on the high school team. Hockey is less likely to be beautiful in that sweet sort of way. Now the skaters *know* their positions, they no longer trip over their own skates, or skate in a clump. Now, there is speed and velocity…and a passion of which a five-year-old has no knowledge. There is a beauty and a *danger*.

To clarify, the danger is not because the skaters skate outside of the rules; danger like that is never beautiful. The beautiful sort of danger comes from *within* the rules. These high school skaters now know the game at a much deeper level than their five-year-old counterparts. Watch the fans and the coaches; the competition is much more intense. In the stands, the atmosphere no longer has the casual feel of watching the five-year-olds' game. Instead, passion has increased in the fans, as well as players. Teamwear abounds, attention becomes *focused*, and even the cheering changes. It is no longer just the cheers of encouragement; instead there is something of the *gut* in it, something of *passion*.

Fast-forward ten more years. One of the high school skaters has made it to the pros. The speed of the skaters and the velocity of the puck have greatly increased. Skaters have a mastery of the rules, their bodies, the puck, the plays. Perhaps the game is a game to make it to the Stanley Cup finals. There are lifelong commitments and dreams on the line. The coaches, the fans, and the skaters are at a heightened level of awareness. Although the rink is still made of ice, there are still two goal nets, there are still skaters with sticks and a puck, there is little else similar to the five-year-olds playing. Now men of elite physical prowess are on the ice. They have brought *everything* to the ice, and that *everything* has everything to do with *passion*.

These men are the virtuosos of hockey, skating with heart and soul. There no longer seem to be individual players; there is instead a *oneness* to the team. To watch them play is to witness beauty—and danger. It is to be caught up and to be involved, investing your own heart and soul. Our cheers are louder, and our collective heartbeat is pounding. And it is *utterly* beautiful and *utterly* dangerous.

✝

"But I'm trying to find something *safe* for my child to do. I don't think my heart can take seeing them in hockey, (or football, or baseball, or fill-in-the-blank). There has to be a way to make hockey safer."

To clarify again, the rules make hockey safe. Breaking the rules makes hockey dangerous in an ugly way, at times, a horrific way. There is no greatness in cheating or breaking rules; and there is no beauty in it. However, to play from *within* the rules is where the beauty comes, accompanied by that passionate danger.

But what if we tried to play a season of *safe hockey?* What if we took the puck away? The puck, although small and, at times, nearly invisible, can be quite dangerous. Skaters get hit by the puck; the goalie *really* gets hit by the puck. There are "fights" over the puck, from the opening face-off to trying to get the puck away from the boards. In those instances alone, there is a flurry of stick-swinging. Hey, why don't we take the sticks away as well? This would really make hockey safe.

Hockey is a game of honor. Why don't we call the skaters to really rely on their honor? They could still be in their teamwear. They could still tryout for the team and their positions. They could still get a really good workout from skating up and down the ice. Hey, they could still do *Herbies*! Everything would be exactly the same: the ice, the uniform, the clock, the fans, the cheers, the coaches, the penalties. You could hardly tell the difference, but it would just be *safe*. The skaters would still participate in the sacrifice of the game, but they would pass, receive, and maneuver the puck *on their honor!* It would still be the same game. Nay, it would be a *better* game, because the whole game would be played according to *honor!*

"I don't get it."

"Well, the skaters would pass the puck *on their honor.*"

"I still don't get it."

"Well, Johnny would pantomime passing the puck to Stephen, who would, in turn, pantomime shooting the puck into the goal."

"How do you know if he scored?"

"Well, the goalie would pantomime the save."

"How do know if the goalie made the save?"

"Well, it would be based on the goalie's *honor.*"

"You're kidding me."

"No. Hockey is game of honor, and the goalie plays hockey, therefore the goalie is honorable. The goalie will honorably say whether or not the save was made."

"Wow! How do you know that you can count on the goalie's honor?"

"Now you're being ridiculous. There would still be referees; they would be able to judge the quality of the pantomimes and make the final call as to a goal, save, or miss. In fact, they would still make all of the same calls on the ice based on the quality of the pantomime."

"What about the fans?"

"What do you mean?"

"Do you think you'll have any? For that matter, do you think that you'll have any skaters?"

"Of course. The fans will still be able to see the skaters getting a workout, there will still be sweat, but there just won't be any missing teeth. No one will get hurt. It won't be dangerous at all."

"Yeah, that's the problem. I would never go to a hockey game like that; it would boring. I'd just go to a baseball game or piano concert."

"Well, they will be safe, too. Baseball will be without the bat and ball—just pantomimed to keep the players safe."

"What about piano? How will you make that 'safe?'"

"Easy. Player pianos."

"You're kidding me."

"No. Player pianos eliminate the danger of mistakes. Mistakes can lead to embarrassment, even a lifetime of shame. The pianist can just pantomime playing the piano. They could even sway. You know, they could pantomime the body movements of the virtuosos."

"I think I would rather get tickets to a competitive thumb wrestling competition, than to watch *any* of your 'safe' competitions."

"Well, that's just silly. Making hockey, or baseball, or piano safe will be better for everyone. It will bring a renewed vitality to the whole thing."

"No it won't. It will *kill* hockey and anything else that you make *safe*."

"I don't see how that would be possible. You are still seeing the great workouts, the great athletes showing their physical prowess."

"That's the thing! I'm not going to see the workout. I'm going to see the game!"

"Well, you would see it. All it would take is a little imagination to enjoy the pantomime."

"What you don't know about hockey is a lot! The 'games' you describe would be *dead*. Hockey is about *life*."

"How could it possibly be 'dead?'"

+

By attempting to make hockey safe and removing the puck, you remove the purpose of the game. Pantomimed hockey on the honor system becomes a subjective exercise in futility. Hockey suddenly is devoid of consequences. There is no puck that actually is slapped across the frozen rink into a net, or caught in the glove of the goalie. Even the most emphatic pantomime has no ramifications. No one would score. Why would the skaters want to leave everything on the ice? Why would they put heart and soul into nothing?

By removing the puck and the consequences of using the puck, the heart and soul are removed. When the heart and soul are gone, there is a death. When *passion* is gone, hockey's beautiful danger is gone. And the beauty of hockey has everything to do with a certain sort of *danger*. Not the danger of breaking the rules, but the *danger of keeping the rules*. When you remove the puck, you contracept hockey, it no longer has anything to do with *life*, but everything to do with *death*.

Relying on *honor* will soon deteriorate. *I* don't even know if I hit the puck. Suddenly, my so-called honor seeks to serve the self, to serve me—I could make a goal whenever I wanted! This will result in chaos, but even the chaos would "deteriorate." After a while, who would even care to argue about the pantomime? Boredom will infect the skaters. Then, the speed of the game will be gone. There will be no reason to skate quickly, as the puck has been removed. The fans will leave. The coaches will need no particular expertise. If the skaters pantomime using the sticks, why can't they pantomime using skates? Why not use cleats? It seems cleats on ice are *safer* than skates on ice. Hey, we could get rid of the ice altogether. Why don't we just draw up the game on paper? We could use a computer program to analyze which team would win each game. And since computers are so fast, we could just analyze which team would win the Cup, and we could give it to them on the first day of the season. This would eliminate a lot of travel and expense—and danger. Hey, why don't we just let people play checkers, but call it hockey? Then everyone could play.

And while I'm on my soapbox, since we will be playing all the games on paper—or checker boards—we won't be needing rinks any longer. We could turn these in to schools, or hospitals, or strip malls. I'm not sure how we could repurpose the Zambonis, but give me some time to think about it.

It all comes down to this: in your attempt to make hockey *safe*, you have contracepted it. By contraception, removing the puck, you take what was passionately beautiful and passionately dangerous and *killed* it. You killed hockey. If it is sterile, it is not clean, it is lifeless.

No man has ever sought the Stanley Cup because he thought it would provide a good workout. No fan watched Herb Brooks and the 1980 USA Men's Olympic Hockey Team in order to learn a few good thigh exercises. It's the *game!* It's *hockey!*

What makes hockey great? When the skaters leave *everything* on the ice, when they give the *full gift of self*, when they skate with *passion* in the fullest sense of the word—this is what makes hockey great.

Hockey is beautiful, and hockey is dangerous. To attempt to remove danger from hockey is for hockey to cease being hockey. Hockey would die, but hockey is for *life*.

We don't often think of a three hundred pound man as being passionate. But the great G.K. Chesterton was just such a man. He understood everything about passion, especially the passion between a man and a woman. "The first two facts which a healthy boy or girl feels about sex are these: first that it is beautiful and then that it is dangerous."[24]

Sex is beautiful, and sex is dangerous, which is why it comes with rules. It is between a husband and wife in marriage. It is to be the *full gift of self*. In other words, it is not to be contracepted. Or sterilized. Sex is to be both unitive and open to procreation. The unitive is the marital embrace. The procreative allows the act to be open to life. Sex that happens outside of the rules—not in marriage, or not unitive, or not open to procreation, or any combination of these—is dangerous, but not dangerous in the beautiful way. Sex that is purposely disconnected from marriage and the possibility of birth, has the same danger as hockey without the puck; it has the danger of *death*.

But sex is about *passion*, and true passion is beautiful *and* dangerous. Which is *why* it comes with rules. Sex has rules in order for it to be about *life*, for "the most dangerous thing in the world is to be alive."[25]

[24] G.K. Chesterton, *Collected Works of G.K. Chesterton*, Volume 28 "The Wrong Books at Christmas" Illustrated London News, Jan. 9, 1909 (San Francisco: Ignatius Press, 1987) 251

[25] G.K. Chesterton, "What is Right with the World," *In Defense of Sanity: The Best Essays of G.K. Chesterton* (San Francisco: Ignatius Press, 2011) 370-371

Chapter Twenty-Seven

THE CUP AND THE ZAMBONI

In North St. Paul, Minnesota, there is a landmark unlike any other. It seems more appropriate to the cold, dark winters of Minnesota, but the landmark stands in season and out of season. The landmark is a 44-foot snowman. I once heard retired Archbishop Flynn say that he always knew how to get to St. Peter's Catholic Church in North St. Paul: "Just take highway 36 east, and take a left at the snowman."

But every snowman has his day, and August 12, 2006 was the day for this snowman. The snowman had a new coat of paint—more correctly, a new sweater of paint. He was now wearing the hockey sweater of the Carolina Hurricanes. Why? There could only be one reason; North St. Paul's favorite son, Bret Hedican, was home with the Stanley Cup. A parade was to take place and *everyone*, even the snowman, must be ready!

In the morning, Bret's children ate their cereal out of the Cup. There was a parade through town to his high school. Later, Bret and the Cup went to his college, then to celebrate with family, then home just to be alone with his wife as they read the names of the many other players who had won the Cup before him. He understood that seeing and touching the Cup moves people. The Cup was taken away at 3 a.m. Bret said that the day was overwhelming and everything for which he had hoped.[26]

---

[26] Hockey Hall of Fame, Stanley Cup Journal 2006, "Bret Hedican," <http://www.hhof.com/html/exSCJ06_25.shtml>

✝

Many years earlier, I had seen pictures of the Stanley Cup when it made another stop in Minnesota. The pictures were from a little neighborhood bar and this time the Cup was being defiled. A descriptive explanation is too much; instead it is enough to say that it was vile. Each time I tell this story there is an audible gasp from the audience, as there should be. Not only do hockey fans gasp, but also non-hockey fans gasp. Everyone understands that the Cup is, in essence, *Hockey*. The Cup is somehow *holy*. To be *holy* is to be *set aside*. The Cup, in fact, has been *set aside*.

The Cup is an icon of the whole story of Hockey. There are over two thousand names written on the cup. The names are from the owners of the teams, staff members and, of course, from the men who played the game and won. These names represent thousands of stories, and the lifelong commitments to a goal. The Cup is the safe-keeper of these stories. In a certain way, the Cup is even the keeper of the stories of the many who never won it. In order for there to be names on the Cup, there must necessarily be names left off the Cup. It is the keeper of the stories of all the moms who know the skate sharpeners, the dads who help tape the sticks, the siblings who cheer at the games, the grandparents who tell stories of the hockey greats from their time. The Cup is *so much more* than just a hunk of metal; it is an *icon*, and it deserves a certain reverence.

The Stanley Cup never arrives at the Championship game tarnished. It never arrives anywhere tarnished. The Cup has been taken all over the world; it has even made trips to Afghanistan to encourage the troops. We expect that the Stanley Cup will always look a certain way—glorious. In fact, we expect ice arenas to look a certain way. Before the game, the ice is untouched and perfect. Who keeps the Cup radiant? Who maintains the rink? Who keeps the surface of the ice perfect? It's the men and women behind the scenes. They prepare everything for the sacrifice of the game; they keep the *shine* on all of hockey—including the Cup. Yes, the Cup is an icon that even tells the stories of the equipment managers, the rink managers, and the Zamboni drivers.

✟

On August 12, 2006 when Bret Hedican took the Cup to his *alma mater*, St. Cloud State, his teammate and fellow alum, Matt Cullen, joined him. They each rode a Zamboni onto the Husky Ice. Who hasn't wanted to drive a Zamboni! As you can imagine, the crowd went wild.

The Zamboni, the slow rolling, lazy giant ice-resurfacing machine usually only makes an appearance when the skaters are gone. What a beautiful juxtaposition this must have been! The Zamboni has a certain sort of storied mystery and there is just *something* about the person who quietly drives the Zamboni. How did they ever get a job driving the Zamboni? There is just *something* in the way the Zamboni resurfaces the ice, making it perfect again.

In hockey, there is a reverence given to the sheet of ice. There is something fantastic in seeing the Zamboni; it is so simple and so beautiful. There can even be a *tug* in the heart to one day drive the Zamboni. In fact, the Zamboni driver is a hero of hockey, an unsung hero, but a hero for preparing the ice for the sacrifice of the game.

Somehow that day, when Bret Hedican and Matt Cullen drove onto the ice on Zambonis, they recapitulated the whole story of hockey. They summed up every single thing for which hockey stands. These two heroes of hockey were driving the machines of hockey's unsung heroes, and in a sense, the men who carried the Cup now carried all the unsung heroes with them. They carried their parents, families, all their coaches, the skate sharpeners, the ice rink managers, the equipment managers, the youth in hockey programs all over the country. They carried with them all those who had gone before them in hockey, all those wounded during the sacrifice of the game, all those who never won anything in hockey. They carried all the fans of every age and of every time; they carried all of hockey. No man wins the Stanley Cup on his own. These two men, these two elite men, who are among just a few thousand men who have won the Cup, *know* that no man wins the Cup on his own. Hedican and Cullen are men of elite physical prowess, yet they were driving hockey's lumbering giant—the Zamboni. In that moment, there was a meeting of the Cup and the Zamboni—a meeting that is omnipresent, but in that moment visible to all.

+

There are unsung heroes in the Church as well. They quietly go about their business all over the world. There are those who quietly feed the poor, quietly visit those sick or imprisoned, quietly clothe the naked. The Catholic Church cares for millions and millions of people each day.

Mary Jo Copeland of Minneapolis is one such hero. Not only does she give out nearly 5,000 meals a week, but she also shelters 500 people a night. She cares for the poor so tenderly, even washing their feet. Once, when praying before a meal, Mary Jo reminded us that no one is ever so poor that he cannot be kind. Just that prayer, from an unsung hero, is a clarion call.

In hockey, some of the unsung heroes care for the skaters, while others care for the ice, the place of the sacrifice. However, hockey understands that caring for the place of the sacrifice *is* caring for the skater. It is the same in the Church. Mary Jo Copeland and so many others care for the human person. In addition, each parish has an Altar and Rosary Society, a maintenance crew, and volunteers who care for the *place* of the sacrifice of the Mass. They are the Zamboni drivers of the Church, quiet and unsung, and caring for others because they care for the place of the Sacrifice.

The same reverence given to the Stanley Cup and the ice should be given to what is holy, holy in the supernatural sense, the Church. This includes not only the physical buildings of Church property, but also the things in them. Each church has been blessed. In addition, the fixtures and items used for Mass have been blessed. They are *holy;* they have been *set aside* and deserve reverence.

The Altar and Rosary Society is in some way mysterious. The roles of its members are nearly always behind the scenes, their duties are done when no one is watching. Among other things, they take care of the linens and vestments of the Mass. There is a very particular way for which the linens must be cared. They are *not* just thrown into the laundry. Instead, they are washed by hand in a particular manner because they have been set aside, because they are holy, and used for the Sacrifice of the Mass.

The rhythm of the Church year dictates different colors and decorations for the altar. In Lent, there may be a particular barrenness about the altar. At Easter, the once-barren altar becomes lush and extravagant in its decorations. Christmas time may find the parish teeming with poinsettias and lighted trees. Ordinary Time finds the altar less adorned. But who is it that does all this work? It's the *spiritual Zamboni drivers.* What does this mean? Volunteers from the parish climb ladders, light trees, water plants. The parish maintenance crew repairs kneelers, changes light bulbs, fixes squeaky doors, repairs the heaters. The youth at my parish thoroughly clean the church each spring. The Altar and Rosary Society clean and care for all the things used at the Mass. There is so much more that goes into the Sacrifice of the Mass than what is seen on Sunday.

Why is this attention paid to the *place*, to the parish? The parish is an icon of the whole Church. The pews in an individual parish have held thousands and thousands of people, a reminder of the millions and millions held by the Church as a whole. Each pew holds the stories of life. A baby has been held there, a toddler has laughed, or been naughty there, a teenager has prepared for Confirmation there, and a widow has mourned her husband there. The pews are the keepers of the stories of our lives.

The walls hold the stories of the greats who have gone before us, the Saints. The statues point to our desire, Christ. The candles are icons of our prayers. Perhaps we see the baptismal font. This, too, is an icon. If this is not the particular font at which we were baptized, it is certainly a symbol of that font. There is only one way into full membership in the Church: through Baptism. Who held us on that day, or stood by us? No one comes to the Church alone.

The doors of the parish are an invitation—not just into a particular parish, but into the Church Universal, into a way of *life*. The aisle is the path, an icon of the path of our lives. Sometimes we will run up the path of life as a carefree child. Other times, we will be bent over, hanging onto the end of each pew as we struggle toward our destination. The Altar is the destination, the place of the Wedding Banquet of the Lamb. It is an icon of heaven. It is a foretaste of what we hope to eternally enjoy. Even our genuflection before the True Presence is an icon of the humility we will show on the day of meeting Christ face-to-face.

Why do people take their time to make certain the purificators are ironed in a particular manner? Why does anyone care if the kneelers are in good repair? Why is it important to have our youth join us as we care for the wood of the pews? Because when we enter the confines of the parish, we are really, in a sense, free of confines. Instead we enter eternity. How wonderful it is that there are men and women and boys and girls who are willing to care for this taste of eternity.

Just as there is a thrill in the possibility of driving the Zamboni, there is a thrill in actually helping with the parish. The Zamboni driver leaves the ice flawless, somehow becoming the perfect host to those who arrive when he is no longer on the rink. The Altar and Rosary Society, the maintenance crew, and the many volunteers leave the parish in a state of utter beauty. They become the perfect hosts to those who come for the Sacrifice of the Mass. They are even the perfect hosts to those who quietly come alone in the middle of a weekday or in the middle of the night. Their loving attention to the parish touches the soul in the pew who may have prayers of thanksgiving, or of sorrow, or of anxiety, or of joy. The spiritual Zamboni drivers understand the importance of what they do, which is why they do it with such care.

For you, too, there is *something* in knowing you have assisted. There is something in knowing that the floors shine brighter because of your handiwork. There is something in knowing that you swept the choir loft. There is something knowing that you helped to repair the leak in the roof. There is something in knowing that you placed the flowers in front of Mary. There is something in assisting not only at the Mass, but also assisting outside of the Mass. To be an unsung hero is good for the soul. Call your Altar and Rosary Society today and see what your parish needs.

You know you have always wanted to drive the Zamboni. Become a *spiritual Zamboni driver.* And at the Mass, when Father holds the Cup, the Chalice—you will finally *see* what has always been. The Cup is the icon of *everything*!

Chapter Twenty-Eight

THE GREAT ONE

Obviously, *The Catechism of Hockey* can *only* lead to one thing: Moses and the Promised Land. But you must have been anticipating this since the second or third chapter. Of course, some of you are saying, "Hey, Moses never went into the Promised Land." If you would, please allow me just a few words about Moses.

Moses led the Israelites to Moab, which was just on the edge of the Promised Land. He would not be leading them any farther because of *one* act of disobedience. We often think that this may be too big of a consequence, but Moses disobeyed God *in front of* all the Israelites. On top of the sin of disobedience, there was the sin of scandal. Because of this, Joshua instead would lead the Israelites to the Promised Land.

At Moab, Moses gives his last lesson to the Israelites. It must have been an amazing time. The Israelites were gathered by Tribe to listen to the man who freed them from slavery to Pharaoh, who had led them through the desert, who had interceded for them, even though they grumbled against him. He had received the Law from God. He had been instrumental in everything they had done for four decades; they counted on Moses for everything. And now he was before them, speaking to them for one last time before they would leave. They knew they would never see Moses again.

"What did he say?"

"It's all laid out in Deuteronomy."

"What is Deuteronomy?"

Deuteronomy is Hebrew for *second law*. In it Moses not only reiterates the Ten Commandments, but he also gives them 610 *new* laws! He knows that the Israelites are a "stiff-necked people," meaning they are stubborn. He knows that they will need additional help if they are to live faithfully in the Promised Land. So, the very last thing Moses does as he speaks to the Israelites on Moab is to *catechize them!*

It seems shocking really. If I were to see my friends and family for the last time, catechizing them seems an unlikely thing to do. I might want to sit in a circle and talk about old times. Remember when…. Maybe we would play a game, or make a scrapbook, or do some kind of craft where we make something to remember each other by. But *Deuteronomy* is not Hebrew for crafting, or face-time, or sharing feelings. Instead, Deuteronomy is Hebrew for second law.

If we think about it, perhaps at the end of our lives we do catechize. I remember what my grandfather told me shortly before he died. "Be good to the people you meet along the way." It was a catechism lesson; he was giving me a *law*. He understood the ramifications of following it, and he understood the ramifications of not following it. He wanted me to *only* follow it so as to never experience the ramifications of not following it. How disappointing it has been when I have not. But what a joy it has been when I have followed his simple law, his simple catechism lesson.

At Moab, Moses has a last *touch* or meeting with the Israelites, and he catechizes them. Then, as though the catechism lesson were not enough, *he imparts a warning.*

In Deuteronomy Moses states:

> Now, Israel, hear the statutes and decrees which I am teaching you to observe, that you may live, and may enter in and take possession of the land which the Lord, the God of your fathers is giving you…. Therefore, I teach you the statutes and decrees as the Lord, my God, has commanded me, that you may observe them in the land you are

entering to occupy…. However, take care and be earnestly on your guard not to forget the things which your own eyes have seen, nor let them slip from your memory as long as you live, but teach them to your children and to your children's children…. (Deut 4: 1,5,9)

Moses plainly *warns* the Israelites to *teach their children.* Who must teach the children? Moses did not say that the Levites, the priests, were responsible for teaching the children. No, instead teaching falls to more than just the priests. The *parents* are to *teach their children.*

A quick run through the Old Testament and you can tell that whenever the Israelites taught their children, things went very well. However, when the Israelites did not teach their children, and generations lost their faith, all hell broke loose—*literally.*

Was Moses just having a crisis of conscience? Was he just being hard on the Israelites because he was not able to enter the Promised Land? Were all these *rules* just a bit much? Was the warning about teaching the children overkill? Lest we think that Moses was a little too strict and maybe going overboard with what God really wanted, things didn't go so badly for Moses after his time on Moab. Yes, he did die, but he died in the friendship of God.

Remember when some of you said that Moses *never* got to go into the Promised Land? Let's flash forward into the story. In the New Testament, Moses is at the Transfiguration, which took place in the land of Israel. Moses *did* reach the Promised Land, just not when he expected to. But what better way to be in the Promised Land than to stand alongside our Savior, Jesus Christ!

+

Well, all that is fine for Moses and the Israelites, but things just aren't like that anymore, and now the children are taught the Faith on Wednesday nights at the parish, which makes the parish responsible.

We may have talked about this before, but let's revisit it one more time. Right before I sat down to write this book, I checked the Rites

Book in the Sacristy. If you want to see it, just ask your pastor; he will be happy to show you.

At the wedding it can be easy to get caught up in the moment. "She just looked so beautiful in that dress!" "He was so handsome and I knew more than ever that he was the one!" The emotions can run high, but the vows are the vows. In the Sacrament of Marriage, the *couple* vows to lovingly accept children from God and to *raise them in the Faith!*

Just in case you were too caught up at the wedding, I double-checked the baptismal vows for words to this effect: "I willingly agree to drop off my children 18 times a year for 75 minutes a week for about eight years, and if Father and the religious education teacher don't get the faith across to my children it is not my fault." Oddly, this is nowhere near what it says.

In the Sacrament of Baptism, the parents are the first to *vow* that *they* will raise their children in the Faith. Next, the Godparents vow the same thing, especially if something should happen that the parents are not able to do it. Finally, the community, which includes the parish, vows to raise the children in the Faith.

The parents *vow*, both at the marriage and at the baptism, that *they* will *teach their children.* Any catechism that happens outside the home is an *added extra bonus.* The pastor and the catechists are *supporting the good work that is happening at home.* Certainly, they may add to the child's catechesis or deepen it, but the catechesis itself is to be taking place at home. This continued action of home catechesis in turn *supports* the catechesis from Father and the parish.

✝

Moses freed the Israelites, and later taught them. But when Moses was first called by God, even he hoped that someone else would do the job. He was not an eloquent speaker, and expected God to find someone more qualified. God assured Moses of His assistance, and that Moses was the man for the job.

Moses was guarding sheep when God called him. He was a regular guy doing a day's work. Being a shepherd is not exactly rich training ground for an important job. Or is it?

Shepherds must know the lay of the land in order to feed their sheep and to find them water. They take cues from their surroundings in order to keep their sheep safe no matter the weather. They must be cunning enough to keep the sheep from predators. All day long, the shepherd is with his sheep. He may be easily lulled into a false sense of safety although at any minute danger may appear. In the black of night, these dangers are ever more present, and the shepherd must remain vigilant. The staff of a shepherd is used in a variety of ways: to defend against predators, to prod his sheep; the hook is used to save the sheep from danger by hooking a sheep by its neck and lifting it out of harm's way. The shepherd has also trained the sheep to recognize his voice, which is especially helpful when multiple herds are together. The act of shepherding requires skill, but it is a quiet skill that perhaps only shepherds appreciate. Shepherds don't normally receive acclaim or distinction.

A man who guards sheep, who is just doing a day's work, whose job can appear to others to be seeming drudgery, who must remain vigilant by day and by night: it sounds like fatherhood. A father is to protect. Even if his job seems like a drudgery to others, he understands the necessity of being vigilant. At times he may have to defend, prod, or save his wayward children. They know his voice and he knows theirs. There is *something* about the *father*.

✝

Even in hockey, there is *something* about the father. The Forward to a simple yellow book called *Hockey for Dummies* states:

> My first experience with a pair of skates and a hockey stick happened
> before I turned three. My coach, also known as "Dad," instructed
> me from the comfort of our kitchen, while I played on the home-
> made rink that had once been our backyard. Dad wasn't trying to

build a hockey star from our kitchen; he was only trying to stay warm. Even back then, hockey was my life. I lived, breathed, slept, dreamed, and played hockey.[27]

Every time I quote this, I ask the audience, "Who said this?" Without fail, and nearly always without hesitation, they say, "Wayne Gretzky." There was even a time that the woman who guessed said that she had never seen a hockey game, but knew who Wayne Gretzky was and that he had to have said it. Wow—the catechesis in hockey is far-reaching!

Yes, Wayne Gretzky did say it, and his moniker is *The Great One*. His *father* was his *first teacher of hockey*. His dad built the rink. Chances are that young Wayne had boundless energy and his dad thought Wayne needed an outlet for it, even in the winter, while his dad could stay warm in the kitchen as Wayne skated. Even in the seemingly simple task of building the rink, Wayne's father was offering a sort of protection to his child. Young Wayne's mind and body were preoccupied with a task under the watchful eye of his father.

There may have been people more qualified to teach young Wayne, but his *dad* taught him first. His dad didn't worry about being the *best* teacher; he just got to the business of teaching. Later his father would introduce Wayne to different, and better, teachers, the coaches, the disciples, but his dad never quit supporting him.

Wayne's father encouraged him to participate in hockey with all his senses, to *live, breathe, sleep, dream, and play hockey*. His father encouraged him to *put on hockey*.

Did Wayne Gretzky's mother support hockey? I think we can safely guess that she took Wayne to more than one practice. She attended more than one game. She knew the skate sharpener by his first name. And she knew the shortest route to every hockey rink in the area.

---

[27] John Davidson and John Steinbreder, Hockey for Dummies (New York: Wiley Publishing, 2000) xxvii.

What if Wayne Gretzky's parents didn't support hockey and his father was not his first teacher? Perhaps he would have picked up hockey at the local rink, but what are the chances that we would call him *The Great One?* Slim, at best. It would be highly unlikely.

What if Wayne Gretzky's mother was his first teacher of hockey and supported him in hockey, and his dad sat in the easy chair with a newspaper and said, "Hockey is for the weak-minded. Just do what your mother says." What if his father didn't go to the games? What if his father refused to watch hockey on television? What if his father mocked his teamwear? What if his father refused to support hockey monetarily? What if his father knew nothing of the rules, or history, or the glory of hockey? What if his father mocked the Stanley Cup? What if his father said, "Do what your mother tells you now, but when you are 16 you can make your own choice."

Now what are the chances we would call Wayne Gretzky the Great One? None. There is no chance he would be called the Great One, and no one will deny it.

There is something about both the mother and father. But there is *something more* about the *father.* Do people try to explain this *something* away? Certainly. Is there a way to quantify this *something?* Not that I know of. But there is *something* about the father.

Mothers and fathers need to teach their children the Faith. And while we must not deny the extraordinary contributions of the mother, when it comes to protection, to teaching, to *catechizing,* there is *something* about the father.

Chapter Twenty-Nine

MORE HOCKEY, PLEASE

Upon my return to the Church, I was surprised by the availability of Catholic teaching. Perhaps my first foray into any sort of Catholic reading took place as I sat in the Adoration chapel. The parish had three or four shelves loaded with books on the lives of the saints, apologetics, Church history, photo essays of beautiful churches around the world, and even some audio books. The books could be checked out, and each week I would leave with a few. I especially liked to listen to the audio books while commuting. At first I wondered, "Where has all this been; why didn't I know this?" Then it became clear—Catholic teaching had always been available. For starters, there was a homily every Sunday. Secondly, there was the Catechism. I just never availed myself of either of these things.

After having discovered the books, I began to realize that my parish and others nearby had speakers that came to teach about some aspect of Catholic teaching. The wildest thing was that the speeches were free! One day I found a Catholic bookstore—it was *loaded* with Catholic books! I used to watch what other people were buying and then choose those books.

It only got better from there. For example, there was a day at Mass when the priest mentioned a Saint in his homily. The name was a complete surprise to me, but I wanted to know more about the Saint and what he taught. So I did something radical for me at that time...I called the priest! Not only did he give me the name of the Saint, he spelled it for me as well, and then told me where I could read more about St. Irenaeus.

The Church is an endless treasure chest!

+

As parents, we often think that it is the responsibility of someone else to form our children in the Faith. We say, "It's really the Church's responsibility to teach the faith." Well, of course, it is the Church's responsibility to teach the Faith, but we are a part of the Church. In making our marriage and baptismal vows, we agreed to assume the responsibility of teaching. Yet, we come back with, "There are people much more qualified to teach our children the Faith; we'll just leave it to the experts so we don't mess anything up." Thank goodness parents don't use this logic when wondering who will teach their child to throw a ball, or to brush their teeth, or to ride a bike, or to skate, or *anything*. Parents are the first teachers!

"Well, it may be fine to teach our children the Sign of the Cross, but we don't really have the time to teach anything else." I once championed the position of I-don't-have-the-time-for (fill-in-the-blank), until I was given the gift of a handy little electronic thing that stored music, could retrieve email, and do a host of other things. Upon getting it, without scheduling time in my so-packed-I-couldn't-possibly-have-time-for-even-one-more-thing calendar, I spent *seven hours* goofing off with it. *SEVEN HOURS—the FIRST day!* I proceeded to take hours each day with it until it taught me the lesson of my life. Making time for something is a discipline. We, in a sense, clear the children's calendars when we purchase another electronic gadget for them. Show me a kid with no time left in the day, give him a new video game, and let's see if this child can't free up a little time out of nowhere to play the game. We clear their schedules and our own for ballet and piano lessons and a host of other activities, especially sports. Well, if there is time for the catechism of ballet, or piano, or soccer, or hockey, there is time for the Catechism of the Catholic Church.

Cal Ahlquist knew the importance of having been the first teacher of his daughter Sarah. Although he was a skater, he knew there were so many other more qualified skaters. But he didn't shy away from his duties; he continued to skate with his daughter throughout her career. Of skating with her, he said, "In your feebleness, if you can help them out in some way, it's a wonderful feeling."

"If we just had the money, we would be able to do a lot more that the parish offers." Although many things at parishes are free, even if there is a fee, the parish will usually offer a reduced rate or even a scholarship. Perhaps one of the most expensive things we have to purchase for our children is a First Communion dress or suit. There certainly are situations of dire need, but often, we find the money for ballet, or piano, or soccer, or hockey. What if we were to reverse the amounts spent on hockey and on our parish?

Often the catechesis of the children falls to one parent, most often the mother. Recently, I spoke with a father who is an amazing provider for his family. He takes his children to Mass, but beyond that, he said, "I try not to get involved in church stuff." My heart broke for him—will he be surprised if his children leave the Faith, will he care? What if Wayne Gretzky's dad took Wayne to the rink, but beyond that "didn't get involved in hockey stuff?" Just as Wayne's dad and Cal Ahlquist taught their children hockey, we must *actively* teach our children the Faith.

But we say, "We just don't have the knowledge." Go get it. Hockey has adult catechesis and so does the Church. The teaching of the Catholic Church is an endless treasure chest; it's waiting for you; open it, and dig in. You will never regret deepening your faith and the faith of your children.

✝

So what happens when we fully catechize our children in hockey? The children don't want less hockey, they want *more!*

A hockey bedroom

A hockey birthday party

Hockey tickets to Gopher and Wild games

Hockey magazines

Hockey books

Hockey websites

Hockey trading cards (which are something like Holy Cards made with hockey players)

More teamwear—not just my team—but the Gophers and the Wild, as well

They want to go to free-skate at the local rink

There is knee hockey (which, by the way, wears out the knees of teamwear sweatpants)

Street Hockey

Table Hockey—or Air Hockey

Broom Ball—which is just hockey with brooms

Hockey video games

Hockey biographies

Hockey statistics

Hockey history

Eventually coaching and refereeing

And eventually, hockey children

They want to live, breathe, sleep, dream, and play hockey!

Hockey is great! I love hockey!

The Church is greater! And what happens if you *fully* catechize your children in the Faith? They want *more.*

A mother of one of my students came to me once. She joked that I had "ruined" her life. Her daughter was now asking to go to Mass early in order to go to confession before Mass. The daughter was now telling the mother and the rest of the family to hurry to get ready. The family now arrives at church early. The mother went on to tell me that she witnessed her own daughter in line for confession and began to wonder why she wasn't there herself. How had I "ruined" the mother's life? She had become complacent and satisfied with not going to confession. Her daughter's faith was on fire, which was a call to the mother, who found herself in line for confession again. There were a few moments of silence in our conversation, then the mother softly said, "Thank you."

Yes, when we *fully* catechize our children, they want *more*.

They want a Crucifix in their rooms

They know how to pray the rosary—and desire to do so

They serve at Mass

They actually listen to the homilies and understand them

In the words of Mitch who is 8-years-old, "My priest gives the best homilies!"

They are not embarrassed to go to donut Sunday or the pancake breakfast put on by the Knights of Columbus

They seek the biographies, the Lives of the Saints (and their Holy Cards)

They understand the rhythm of the Church Calendar

They are happy to go to the Fish Fry during Lent

They go to the Stations of the Cross

They come to understand the history of the world and the vast influence of the Church

They desire pilgrimages

They come to understand the Mass

They go to Adoration

They desire the Sacraments

They come to understand Scripture

They wear Catholic teamwear—not just the scapular, but a medal of a Saint, and a t-shirt from the retreat they went on

They seek out retreats

They come to understand that "me, me, me," is not the way to look at the world

They will help with the parish cookbook, bazaar, and fundraising bake sales

They begin to serve in their parishes with volunteer work

They begin to serve their families—not expecting to be served

They learn how to *think*—*logically*

They come to love the Church and Her teaching

They come to respect the priesthood and the religious life

They see the Faith as infused in everything

They seek ways to be faithful in college

They respect the dignity of women—and men

They respect the dignity of the unborn and are unashamed to pray for the unborn

They go to marriage in a state of grace and purity

They lovingly accept children and raise them in the Faith

They *fully* catechize their children

They raise a new generation who live, breathe, sleep and dream their Faith

They seek this all for the Eternal Crown of Glory for themselves and for their children

As parents, you have eternal souls on your hands. Perhaps there is a future Stanley Cup parent reading now. Imagine your pride as a parent. I would *love* to come to that parade.

But as parents, your responsibility is to get the eternal souls entrusted to you to heaven. The Eternal Crown of Glory is available to all your children. You *must* give them the tools to receive the Crown—you must catechize them. You will be held responsible if your child has not been given the Faith.

Imagine being next to your Maker when He meets your child and He says to your child, "Well done, good and faithful servant." Imagine your pride! Imagine your joy! Imagine the *beauty* of your child receiving the Eternal Crown of Glory. You never want to miss this, so give them the Way.

✝

Moses has a particular place in my heart. Certainly, I can see myself as one of the people who would have grumbled against him. Certainly, I would have been quick to break the Ten Commandments and later the other 610 laws. But his steadfastness would have continually called me home. In fact, his steadfastness continually calls me home today. But it's that last speech on Moab; the last time the Israelites would see him. My heart breaks with theirs; somehow, in the Exodus story, Moses has become my friend.

Moses reiterated the Ten Commandments, gave the Israelites new laws, and then imparted a warning to *teach your children*. If I may be so bold, I would like to add to what Moses has said:

Teach your children the Faith...as if it were hockey!

ACKNOWLEDGMENTS

Sometimes I think about strange things. Sunday night, March 11, 2007 was no exception. I was pondering *why* sports have become a religion. In what must surely be one of the very much lesser gifts of the Holy Spirit, I received my answer in what can only be described as a *poof.* In that moment, I had nearly the complete *Catechism of Hockey.* My greatest thanks are to the Third Person of the Blessed Trinity.

Beyond my faith, perhaps one of my most favorite gifts is that of seeing things through analogy. My late father often explained things by analogies. As a catechist, I reach for them constantly to impart the Faith. Whenever speaking of my own father, I cannot help but think also of my spiritual father, the late Bishop Paul Dudley. One day, when I was relating how I came to understand a certain Catholic teaching, I repeated to him the analogy that finally made it clear. He said in his beautiful breathy voice, "Imagine, even an old bishop like me can learn something new!" Without these two men, there would be nothing, no me; they each gave me life. *The Catechism of Hockey* is a thank you to them.

Then there is my dear friend Ellie. She called that first night to tell me of her engagement; instead she was subjected to the first lecture on the Catechism of Hockey. Thank you for your patience and prayers.

My technical advisor concerning hockey was Mr. Jake Halsne. He finished his high school career in hockey as I finished the book.

I'm so grateful for the many out-of-blue phone calls he fielded to clarify nuances of the rules and the game.

Over the years of speaking about hockey and the Faith, people would ask, "What are you going to do with the Stanley Cup?" or "How will you work the Zamboni into it?" People would tell me their hockey stories, many of them bloody. There was always a joy in their eyes as they spoke. I've tried to answer all the questions, and have incorporated many of the stories into this book. Thank you to those who had questions, and for trusting me with your stories.

One of the most beautiful stories that was entrusted to me was that of Cal and Sarah. After Dale Ahlquist read the second draft, he told me, "I'm sorry, but you need to write more. There is another story that has to be in the book." He introduced me to his brother Cal Ahlquist. Speaking with Cal felt like spending time with a mystic. After interviewing him, he made me the best pizza and best broasted potatoes at his shop, The Pizza Factory. Later, I interviewed Sarah Ahlquist. She was just as wonderful! Dale was right—they *had* to be in the book. Thank you for your story.

Then there are the many readers. Thank you especially to Laura Ahlquist and Emily de Rotstein. Thank you to those who helped me edit, especially Therese Warmus, and to my students Hannah and Rose Korman.

This is the book of four shoulder surgeries. My sister, Karla, and a million friends saw to my health in this time. Thank you for getting me through.

There are two family members without whom this would never have been possible. My mother always asked about the progress, and always encouraged me. Thank you for my life, thank you for your sacrifice, thank you for your love. And my brother John. Everyone should have a brother John. Your generosity mirrors Dad's generosity. He would be so proud of you, and so grateful to you.

And then there is Dale Ahlquist. We met in 2008, so it has been really only five years that he has waited for the book, not the six years he claims. Five years, six years—these are the arguments we love to have. He has been entirely too good to me for all these years. He understands my quirks, he allows me such freedom, and he sees promise. Without Dale, I would still have to hear people asking me how the book is coming. Because of Dale, you are holding it in your hands. He is a dreamer that always does what he dreams. I once asked his wife, Laura, about how this was possible. She explained, "He is never afraid to look like a fool for having done what he is called to do." Ah—yes, Dale Ahlquist is a fool—he is a fool for Christ! Thank you for *everything* these past five or six years.